Indian Cookbook

Authentic and Traditional 60 Indian Recipes to Try at Home

Sahil Batra

Table of Contents

EGG CURRY (ANDEY KI CURRY)

Total: 40 mins
Prep: 10 mins
Cook: 30 mins
Yield: Serves 2 to 3 people

Ingredients
6 hard-boiled eggs
5 tbsp. cooking oil (vegetable, canola, or sunflower)
2 medium-sized onion (cut into □uarters)
3 medium-sized tomatoes (cut into quarters)
2 green chilies
2 tsp. garlic paste
2 tsp. ginger paste
2 tsp. coriander powder
1 tsp. cumin powder
1 tsp. garam masala powder
1/2 tsp. turmeric powder
1/2 tsp. red chili powder
Salt to taste
Optional: 2 potatoes cut into 1-inch cubes
To Garnish: Chopped fresh coriander leaves

To Garnish: 2 green chilies, slit lengthwise

Steps to Make It

Heat 2 tbsp. of the cooking oil in a deep pan and when hot, add the onions. Fry till slightly golden. Turn off the fire. Use a slotted spoon to remove the onions from the pan and put them in a food processor. Grind the onions, tomatoes, and green chilies into a smooth paste. Try not to add water while grinding, if possible.

Heat the remaining oil in the same pan and add the paste you just made. Fry for 2 to 3 minutes.

Add the ginger and garlic pastes, all the dry spices (coriander powder, cumin powder, garam masala powder, turmeric powder, and red chili powder) then mix and fry till the oil begins to separate from the masala (onion-tomato-spice mix).

Add 2 cups of warm water to this masala and bring to a boil on a medium flame.

If adding potatoes to the curry, add them now and cook till half done.

Half slit the boiled eggs vertically and add them gently to the gravy. Simmer the flame and cook for 10 minutes or till the gravy has thickened or reduced to about 3/4 of the original ☐uantity (before you added the water). If you have added potatoes they should ideally be cooked by now.

Turn off the fire and garnish with chopped coriander leaves and the slit green chilies (if using). Serve hot with plain boiled Basmati rice and a vegetable side dish.

☐

JEERA RICE (CUMIN RICE)

Total: 35 mins
Prep: 5 mins
Cook: 30 mins
Yield: 2 to 3 servings

Ingredients
1 cup Basmati rice (a long grain Indian rice)
3 cups water
Salt to taste
2 tablespoons vegetable, sunflower or canola oil/ghee
1 large onion (finely chopped)
2 teaspoons cumin seeds
1/2 cup water
Coriander leaves to garnish

Steps to Make It
Wash the Basmati rice well in running water.
Add the 3 cups of water and salt to taste to the rice and set it up to boil.

Once the rice is almost cooked (test a few grains often to check—they will feel soft on the outside but very slightly hard on the inside), remove from fire and drain the water by straining the rice through a sieve or colander. Set aside.

In another pan, heat the oil/ghee till hot and add onions.

Fry till light brown and then add the cumin seeds. The seeds will splutter and sizzle to show they are done.

Now add the rice and stir well.

Add 1/2 a cup of water to the rice and cover.

Simmer till all the water dries up.

Allow the rice to stand for another 2 to 3 minutes and then serve garnished with coriander leaves.

Enjoy!

PUNJABI-STYLE CHOLE CHICKPEA CURRY RECIPE

Total: 65 mins
Prep: 20 mins
Cook: 45 mins
Yield: 4 servings

Ingredients
3 large onions (sliced thin, divided)
2 large tomatoes (chopped)
1 tablespoon ginger paste
2 tablespoons garlic paste
2 tablespoons vegetable oil (or canola or sunflower cooking oil)
2 bay leaves
5 to 6 cloves

3 to 4 green cardamoms
5 to 6 peppercorns
1 teaspoon cumin powder
2 teaspoons coriander powder
1/2 teaspoon red chili powder
1/4 teaspoon turmeric powder
2 teaspoons garam masala
2 cans of chickpeas
Kosher salt (to taste)
Water (enough to make a gravy)
1-inch piece of ginger (julienned)
2 tablespoons fresh coriander leaves (chopped fine)

Steps to Make It
Gather the ingredients.
Grind 2 of the sliced onions, the tomatoes, and the ginger and garlic paste together into a smooth paste in a food processor.
Heat the vegetable oil in a deep, thick-bottomed pan on medium heat.
Add the bay leaves, cloves, cardamom, and peppercorns and sauté until slightly darker and mildly fragrant.
Add the remaining sliced onion and fry until light golden in color.
Add the onion-tomato paste you made earlier and fry till the oil begins to separate from the paste.
Add the dry, powdered spices—cumin, coriander, red chili, turmeric, and garam masala powders. Sauté, stirring fre□uently, for 5 more minutes.
Drain the water in the can from the chickpeas and rinse them well under running water.
Now add the chickpeas to the masala you fried up earlier. Stir to mix everything well.
Add salt to taste and enough hot water to make the gravy—about 1 1/2 cups.
Simmer and cook covered for 10 minutes.
Use a flat spoon or potato masher to mash some of the chickpeas coarsely. Stir to mix everything well.
Garnish with juliennes of ginger and finely chopped fresh coriander leaves. A s□ueeze of lemon and a handful of very finely chopped onion tastes great as a garnish too.
Serve hot and enjoy!
□

PALAK PANEER (SPINACH AND COTTAGE CHEESE)

Total: 40 mins
Prep:15 mins
Cook: 25 mins
Yield: Servings 6 to 8

Ingredients
1 pound/500 gms paneer (look below for recipe to make your own paneer)
2 medium-sized bunches of spinach (fresh, approximately 1 lb. or 500 gm.)
1/2 bunch fresh fenugreek leaves (approximately 1/4 lb./125 gms)
4 tbsp. vegetable oil (or canola/sunflower oil)
1 large onion (chopped fine)
1 large tomato (diced)
2 teaspoons garlic paste

1 teaspoon ginger paste
2 teaspoons coriander powder
1 teaspoon cumin powder
1/2 teaspoon turmeric powder
1 teaspoon garam masala powder
Salt to taste
Garnish: 1 tbsp. of butter

Steps to Make It
Cut the paneer into 1" cubes. Heat 2 tbsps of oil in a heavy-bottomed pan and stir-fry the paneer till golden. Remove and drain on paper towels. Keep aside.
Add 2 tbsps of oil to the same pan and fry the onions in it till soft.
Add the ginger and garlic pastes and fry for a minute.
Add the spinach, fenugreek leaves, tomato, coriander, cumin, turmeric, and garam masala powders and mix well. Add salt to taste and mix well.
Cook till the spinach and fenugreek leaves are soft and like pulp. Mash well into a rough paste. If you prefer, you can also blend this paste in the food processor to get a smoother consistency.
Add the previously fried paneer cubes to this gravy and mix to coat the pieces.
Garnish with butter and serve hot with Chapatis (Indian flatbread), parathas (pan-fried Indian flatbread) or Makki Ki Roti (pan-fried maize bread).
☐

ALOO MATAR GOBI

Total: 40 mins
Prep: 20 mins
Cook: 20 mins
Yield: 3 servings

Ingredients
2 cups cauliflower florets (fresh or frozen)
Dash of salt (or to taste)
2 large or 3 medium-sized potatoes (peeled or unpeeled, washed and cut into 1-inch cubes)
3 tablespoons vegetable oil (or canola or sunflower oil)
1 teaspoon cumin seeds
1 large onion (finely chopped)
2 teaspoons garlic paste
1 teaspoon ginger paste
2 teaspoons coriander powder
1 teaspoon cumin powder
1/2 teaspoon turmeric powder

1/2 teaspoon red chili powder
2 large tomatoes (finely chopped)
Optional: 2 green chilies (slit lengthwise)
1 cup shelled peas (fresh or frozen)
Fresh coriander (chopped)

Steps to Make It

Thoroughly clean the cauliflower. If using fresh cauliflower, put the florets in a large bowl and cover them with hot water. Add a teaspoon of salt and mix well. Keep aside for 10 minutes.

Put the potatoes in a microwave-safe dish and cover them with hot water. Add salt to taste and mix well. Cook on high for three to four minutes. You can also do this in a pan on the stove top. Cook the potatoes until they are par-boiled. Drain the water and set the potatoes aside.

Heat the cooking oil in a deep, heavy-bottomed pan on a medium flame. When the oil is hot, add the cumin seeds and cook them until the spluttering stops.

Now add the onion and fry it until it is soft. Stir the ingredients often. Add the ginger and garlic pastes now and fry everything for one minute.

Add all the spices and fry everything for another minute. Now add the chopped tomatoes and green chilies (if using). Stir well and fry till tomatoes start to get soft (about two to three minutes).

Now add the cauliflower florets, potatoes, and peas. Stir everything well. Add salt to taste. Cover the pan and cook everything for three to five minutes. Turn off the heat.

Garnish the meal with chopped fresh coriander and serve it with hot chapatis or parathas. Naan or rotis are also good accompaniments.

☐

MUTTER MUSHROOM KI SUBZI

Total: 25 mins
Prep: 10 mins
Cook: 15 mins
Yield: 4 Portions (4 Servings)

Ingredients
1 cup green peas (fresh or frozen)
About 1 pound/500 g. button mushrooms (cleaned and cut into □uarters)
1 large onion (chopped finely)
2 cloves garlic (chopped finely)
1/2 tsp. turmeric powder
1/2 tsp. cumin seeds
1/2 tsp. red chili powder
2 tbsp. vegetable cooking oil (or canola or sunflower oil)
Garnish: coriander (fresh, chopped)

Steps to Make It
Heat the cooking oil in a deep pan, on a medium flame. When hot, add the cumin seeds
and fry till spluttering stops.
Add the garlic and fry till pale golden. Now add the onions and fry till soft.

Add the peas and mushrooms and the powdered spices. Add salt to taste and cook till the mushrooms begin to give off their juices. Stir occasionally. Turn off the fire.
Garnish with chopped coriander and serve with hot Chapatis (Indian flatbread) or Parathas (pan-fried Indian flatbread).

SPICY MINCED MEAT KHEEMA PARATHA

Total: 45 mins
Prep: 15 mins
Cook: 30 mins
Yield: 4 to 6 servings

Ingredients
3 cups whole wheat flour
1 cup water (approximately)
2 cups masala kheema
2 tablespoons ghee (clarified butter, approximately)

Steps to Make It
Prepare the Paratha
Adding just a little water at a time, knead the whole-wheat flour into a smooth, medium-soft dough. It is likely that you will not need the full cup of water.
Place the dough in a bowl, cover with plastic wrap a clean towel, and set aside for one hour.
In the meantime, prepare the masala kheema according to the recipe or allow your leftovers to reach room temperature.
Divide the dough into e☐ually sized balls, about the size of a golf ball.

Lightly flour a clean surface and roll each ball out into a circle that is about 3 inches in diameter.

Place approximately 1 1/2 tablespoons of the masala kheema in the center of the dough and fold the edges over to cover the filling completely. Gently press to seal.

Roll the dough out into a circle of 7 to 8 inches in diameter. For convenience sake, roll out as many parathas as you like. Stack them with a layer of cling film between each paratha so they're ready to cook.

Fry the Paratha

With your paratha prepared, you will fry them one at a time. If you do not have ghee, olive oil is a good substitute.

Heat a griddle and place one paratha on it.

When you see tiny bubbles rise to the surface, flip it over.

Immediately after the first flip, about 3/4 teaspoon ghee on the top of the paratha and spread it all over the surface.

Fry for 30 seconds and flip again. Drizzle ghee on this side as well.

Flip once again to fry the other side. The paratha is done when both sides are crispy and golden brown.

Continue these steps until all of your kheema parathas are cooked.

INDIAN MASALA KHEEMA (DRY SPICY MINCED MEAT)

Total: 25 mins
Prep: 5 mins
Cook: 20 mins
Yield: 4 servings

Ingredients
3 tablespoons vegetable oil (or canola or sunflower cooking oil)
1 teaspoon cumin seeds
2 medium onions (finely chopped)
1 tablespoon garlic paste
1 tablespoon ginger paste
2 tablespoons coriander
1 tablespoon cumin
1 tablespoon garam masala
Salt (to taste)
1 pound ground beef (or use any ground meat you prefer for this recipe)
2 medium tomatoes (finely chopped)
1/2 lime (or lemon, juiced)
Garnish: fresh cilantro leaves (chopped)

Steps to Make It

Gather the ingredients.

Heat the cooking oil in a wok or deep pan over medium heat.

Add the cumin seeds and fry for 1 minute or until the seeds stop spluttering.

Add the onions and sauté till they turn a pale golden color - about 5 minutes.

Add the garlic and ginger pastes and fry for 1 minute to get rid of the "raw" fragrance.

Add the coriander, cumin, garam masala, and salt to taste and sauté, stirring almost continuously, until the oil begins to separate from the masala. (When this happens, you know the spices are cooked to perfection.)

Add the meat to the masala and sauté until browned, stirring often to prevent burning - about 5 to 7 minutes.

Add the tomatoes, stir, and cook until they are soft.

Turn off the heat, add the lime or lemon juice, and stir to mix well.

Garnish with chopped coriander leaves and serve hot.

Enjoy!

CHICKEN SAAGWALA

Total: 40 mins
Prep: 10 mins
Cook: 30 mins
Yield: 4 to 6 servings

Ingredients
2.2 pounds kinless chicken pieces (legs or breasts preferable)
3 large bunches spinach
3 tablespoons vegetable cooking oil
5 peppercorns
4 cloves
4 pods cardamom
2 large onions (chopped very fine)
2 tablespoons garlic paste
1 tablespoon ginger paste
1/2 teaspoon ground turmeric
1/2 ground cinnamon
1 teaspoon coriander powder
1 teaspoon cumin powder
1 tablespoon garam masala powder
2 medium tomatoes (chopped fine)
Garnish: 1 dollop of butter
Optional: Salt to taste

Steps to Make It

Wash the spinach well and chop. Put into a pot with half a cup of water, salt to taste, and boil till cooked.

Grind the spinach into a paste in a food processor. Keep aside.

Heat the oil in a pan on a medium flame and fry the chicken pieces until well browned. Remove and keep aside.

Again heat the same oil, then add the whole spices.

As the spices turn slightly darker, add the onion, ginger and garlic pastes and fry till the onions are pale golden in color.

Add all the other spices: coriander, cumin, and garam masala. Fry for 5 minutes.

Add the tomatoes and fry till the oil begins to separate from the masala.

Add the chicken to this masala, mix well, and add half a cup of water. Cook till the chicken is almost done.

Add the spinach and mix well. Cook until most of the water dries up. Remove from the fire and garnish with a dollop of fresh butter.

Serve with hot chapatis (Indian flatbread

FISH AMRITSARI

Total: 18 mins
Prep: 10 mins
Cook: 8 mins
Yield: Serves 4

Ingredients
1 kilogram fish (any fish with firm, white flesh) cut into medium-thick slices
3 tablespoons ginger paste
3 tablespoons garlic paste
1 teaspoon turmeric powder
1 teaspoon coriander powder
1 teaspoon cumin powder
1 teaspoon carom seeds (ajwain)
1 teaspoon chili powder
Dash salt to taste
2 tablespoons lime juice (juice of 1 lime)
1 1/2 cups Bengal gram flour
Oil to shallow fry fish
Juice of 1 lemon
1 lime (wedged)

Steps to Make It

Mix all the ingredients except the fish and lime wedges, in a large, shallow dish. Form a thick paste.

Gently fold the fish into this paste, making sure to coat each piece well. Allow to marinate for 1 hour.

In a wide, flat pan, heat enough oil to shallow fry the fish till each piece is golden and crisp on both sides.

Serve hot, arranged in a platter. Squeeze lemon juice over the pieces just before serving. Garnish with lime wedges.

LACHCHA PARATHA (LAYERED INDIAN BREAD)

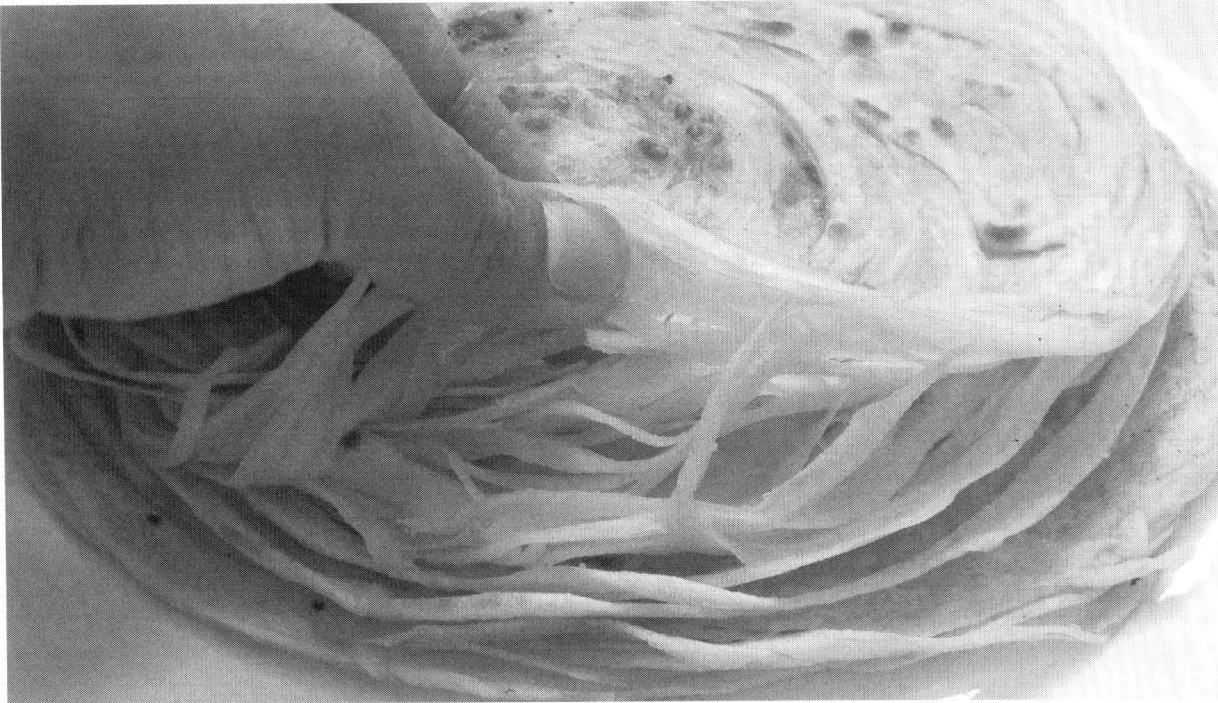

Total: 30 mins
Prep: 20 mins
Cook: 10 mins
Yield: 6 to 8 servings

Ingredients
2 cups whole wheat flour (divided)
3/4 cup water (or more, as needed) to make the dough
Salt to taste
1 cup ghee (clarified butter, divided)

Steps to Make It
Gather the ingredients.
Mix the flour and salt and knead into a soft dough with a little water at a time. Set aside.
Mix 3 tablespoons ghee with 1 tablespoon flour, and set aside.
Divide the dough into e□ually sized balls. Divide each ball into 2 portions.
Take each portion and roll into a long, finger-thick noodle shape.
Coil the first shape into a spiral.
Flour a rolling surface lightly and very gently roll out the spiral into a flat circle about 5 inches in diameter (1/3 inch thick).
Grease the top surface with the ghee-flour mix.
Roll the next shape in the same way and place over the first circle. This makes one Lachcha Paratha. Repeat with the remaining dough.

Heat a flat pan on medium heat.

Fry each paratha as follows: After placing it on the pan the first time, turn after 30 seconds. Spread ghee on the top surface and turn again. Grease the side now on top. Turn often and fry until crisp and golden.

Serve and enjoy!

JALEBI

Total: 115 mins
Prep: 25 mins
Cook: 90 mins
Yield: Serves 4-6

Ingredients
Batter Ingredients:
2 cups flour (self-raising)
1/2 teaspoon baking powder
1 cup yogurt
3 strands saffron
1/4 teaspoon cardamom powder
3 inches vegetable oil (canola/sunflower cooking oil for deep frying)
2 drops food coloring (orange)
Syrup Ingredients:
1 cup sugar
2 tablespoons rosewater

Steps to Make It
Gather the ingredients.
Mix the flour, baking powder, yogurt, and food coloring into a batter and keep aside for 24 hours to ferment.
Pour batter into a ketchup dispensing bottle.

To make sugar syrup, melt the sugar with the rosewater in a small saucepan and boil to get a one thread consistency. To check for one thread consistency, carefully dip the tip of your index finger into the syrup, touch your finger and thumb together and gently tease apart. If one thread is formed between your finger and thumb, the syrup is done.

Turn off the fire, add the saffron strands and cardamom and stir well.

Heat the oil in a deep wok-like dish. To test for the right temperature, drop a small amount of batter into the oil. If it sizzles and rises to the top of the oil, the oil is hot enough. Keep the flame on medium at all times to ensure thorough cooking of the jalebis.

Now hold the ketchup dispenser over the hot oil and s□ueeze the batter into the oil into a wiggly, randomly coiled circle. Squeeze out several at a time.

Fry till light golden and then remove and put directly into the sugar syrup.

Allow to soak for 2 to 3 minutes and then remove.

Serve warm.

IDLIS STEAMED RICE CAKES

Total: 40 mins
Prep: 20 mins
Cook: 20 mins
Yield: 4-6 portions (4-6 servings)

Ingredients
3 cups rice
1 cup skinless urad daal (black gram)
Salt to taste
2 tablespoons vegetable, canola or sunflower cooking oil

Steps to Make It
Wash the rice and lentils separately and soak them overnight.
Grind each separately, into thick pastes (adding a little water at a time) in a blender.
Mix the pastes together and add salt to taste.
Set the batter aside overnight to ferment.
Grease the molds on an idli tray with cooking oil. Pour enough batter into each mold to fill it three-fourths full.
Pour 2 cups of water into a large pot and heat. Put the idli tray into the pot and steam for 20 minutes.
Check the idlis by poking each with a toothpick. If it comes out clean, they are done.

Serve piping hot with sambar or South Indian coconut chutney.

CURD RICE (SOUTH INDIAN YOGURT RICE)

Total: 80 mins
Prep: 60 mins
Cook: 20 mins
Yield: 2 to 4 servings

Ingredients
1 cup rice
2 1/2 cups water
1 cup sour yogurt
Salt to taste
3 tbsp. vegetable, canola or sunflower oil
1 tsp. mustard seeds
5 to 6 curry leaves
3 dry red chilies
Coriander (cilantro) leaves for garnish

Steps to Make It
Wash the rice well and put in a pressure cooker with the water. Cook until done--cook
first on high heat until you hear the first whistle, then simmer and allow 1 more whistle.
Set aside for 1 to 2 hours.
Mix the yogurt into the rice and add salt to taste.
Heat the oil in a small pan and add the mustard seeds, curry leaves, and dry red chilies.
Cook until the chilies are almost black.
Add this mix to the rice and stir well. Garnish with coriander leaves.
Serve with a pickle or chutney.

VEGAN INDIAN CAULIFLOWER CURRY

Total: 35 mins
Prep: 10 mins
Cook: 25 mins
Yield: 3 Servings

Ingredients
1 1/2 teaspoon fresh ginger, grated
2 tablespoons sesame seeds
3 tablespoons peanuts
3 cloves garlic, minced
1 tablespoon cumin
1 teaspoon ground cloves
1 teaspoon turmeric
1/2 teaspoon cayenne pepper
2 tablespoon water
1 tablespoon vegetable oil
2 onions, diced
1 cauliflower, chopped
1 1/2 tablespoon lemon juice

Steps to Make It

Gather the ingredients.

In a blender or food processor, grind together the ginger, sesame seeds, peanuts, garlic, spices, and water.

Sautee the onions in vegetable oil in a pan over medium-high heat, about three to five minutes, or until onions turn clear.

Add cauliflower and spices mixture to the pan and cover.

Allow it to cook another 10 to 12 minutes, occasionally stirring until cauliflower is almost fully cooked.

Add lemon juice and allow to cook for 3 more minutes.

Serve and enjoy!

BUND GOBHI/ PATTA GOBHI KI SUBJI (STIR FRY CABBAGE)

Total: 25 mins
Prep: 10 mins
Cook: 15 mins
Yield: 4 servings

Ingredients
1 medium/250-300 gram cabbage (sliced very thinly)
Optional: 2 medium potatoes (quartered lengthwise and then sliced thinly)
Optional: 1 cup frozen peas (or fresh peas)
2 tbsps vegetable/canola/sunflower cooking oil
5-6 curry leaves
1/2 tsp. mustard seeds

2 green chilies (chopped fine)
2-inch piece ginger (grated)
2 large tomatoes (cut into 1-inch cubes)
1/2 tsp turmeric powder
1 tsp coriander powder
1 tsp cumin powder
1 tsp red chili powder (use less for less spicy)
Salt to taste
Fresh coriander for garnish (chopped)

Steps to Make It

Heat the oil in a pan on a medium flame. Add the mustard seeds, green chilies, curry leaves and fry till the seeds stop spluttering.

Add the ginger and stir. Add the tomatoes and cook till they are pulpy.

If you are using peas and potatoes, add them now. Cook for 4-5 minutes. Add the cabbage and then the turmeric, coriander, cumin, red chili powder and salt to taste. Mix well.

Cover, simmer and cook for 10 minutes.

Garnish with freshly chopped coriander and serve with hot Chapatis (Indian flatbread) and a tangy pickle.

□

PALAK PANEER (SPINACH AND COTTAGE CHEESE)

Total: 40 mins
Prep: 15 mins
Cook: 25 mins
Yield: Servings 6 to 8

Ingredients
1 pound/500 gms paneer (look below for recipe to make your own paneer)
2 medium-sized bunches of spinach (fresh, approximately 1 lb. or 500 gm.)
1/2 bunch fresh fenugreek leaves (approximately 1/4 lb./125 gms)
4 tbsp. vegetable oil (or canola/sunflower oil)
1 large onion (chopped fine)
1 large tomato (diced)
2 teaspoons garlic paste
1 teaspoon ginger paste
2 teaspoons coriander powder
1 teaspoon cumin powder
1/2 teaspoon turmeric powder
1 teaspoon garam masala powder
Salt to taste
Garnish: 1 tbsp. of butter

Steps to Make It

Cut the paneer into 1" cubes. Heat 2 tbsps of oil in a heavy-bottomed pan and stir-fry the paneer till golden. Remove and drain on paper towels. Keep aside.

Add 2 tbsps of oil to the same pan and fry the onions in it till soft.

Add the ginger and garlic pastes and fry for a minute.

Add the spinach, fenugreek leaves, tomato, coriander, cumin, turmeric, and garam masala powders and mix well. Add salt to taste and mix well.

Cook till the spinach and fenugreek leaves are soft and like pulp. Mash well into a rough paste. If you prefer, you can also blend this paste in the food processor to get a smoother consistency.

Add the previously fried paneer cubes to this gravy and mix to coat the pieces.

Garnish with butter and serve hot with Chapatis (Indian flatbread), parathas (pan-fried Indian flatbread) or Makki Ki Roti (pan-fried maize bread).

☐

DHOKLA RECIPE (STEAMED GRAM FLOUR SNACK)

Total: 4 hrs
Prep: 3 hrs 30 mins
Cook: 30 mins
Yield: 4 Portions (4 Servings)

Ingredients
1 bag/500 g. Bengal gram flour (Besan)
1 1/2 cup sour yogurt
1 tsp. ginger paste
1 tsp. green chili paste (add more if you like it spicier)
2 tbsp. sugar
1/2 tsp. turmeric powder
1 tsp. lime or lemon juice
2 tbsp. fruit salt or baking soda
Salt to taste
For tempering: 2 tbsp. vegetable or canola or sunflower cooking oil
1 tsp. black mustard seeds
1 tsp. sesame seeds
6 to 8 curry leaves
2 green chilies slit lengthwise
1/2 cup warm water
For garnish: 1/2 cup finely chopped fresh coriander leaves

Steps to Make It

Sieve the gram flour. Mix it with the yogurt and keep aside for 2 hours.

Add the ginger and green chili pastes, turmeric powder salt to taste, lime juice and sugar and enough warm water to make a batter of pouring consistency. Mix well.

Divide the batter into three e☐ual portions.

Prepare the steamer and grease a square or rectangular pan to steam the Dhokla in.

Divide the fruit salt/baking soda into three e☐ual portions and add one portion to a portion of the batter. Mix well. Pour this batter into the greased dish and put it into the steamer.

Cook till done - when you touch the surface of the Dhokla your fingers should come away clean.

Repeat with the remaining batter, adding the fruit salt/ baking soda to each batch of batter just before steaming.

Allow the steamed dhokla to cool slightly and cut into 2-inch squares.

To temper, heat the oil in a wide, thick-bottomed pan and add the curry leaves, mustard and sesame seeds and green chilies. Fry till the seeds stop sputtering. Pour these into the warm water. Sprinkle this mixture all over the prepared dhokla. Keep aside for 10 minutes.

Garnish with the chopped coriander and serve with tamarind chutney and mint-coriander chutney.

MOONG DAAL KA CHEELA - SAVORY MOONG BEAN PANCAKES

Total: 90 mins
Prep: 45 mins
Cook: 45 mins
Yield: 8 Bean Pancakes (serves 4)

Ingredients
2 cups split moong lentils without skin - see link below for a picture of Moong
2 dry red chilies
1 teaspoon cumin seeds
1/4 teaspoon asafetida powder
2-inch piece of ginger, finely grated
2 finely chopped green chillies (optional)
1/2 cup finely chopped fresh coriander
Salt to taste
Vegetable, canola or sunflower oil (for frying)

Steps to Make It
Thoroughly wash the Moong under running water. Put it into a large bowl and add the dry red chillies, cumin seeds and asafetida powder. Mix well and add enough warm water to cover the Moong fully. Leave overnight to soak.

The next morning, drain the water away, grind the moong and spices you soaked with it, in a food processor to get a fine paste. Add water only as required to get the consistency of pancake batter - thick but 'pour-able'. Add the grated ginger, chopped coriander and salt to taste and mix well.

Heat a griddle or heavy-bottomed pan on medium heat. When hot, add a few drops of cooking oil to it and swirl to coat all sides of the pan. Now pour a ladle full of batter onto the pan and lightly use the ladle to spread the batter into a circular shape from the center outwards. Make a circle of diameter roughly 6 inches. Cook for 1 minute.

Drizzle with a little oil and lift the edges of the Cheela to allow oil to go under it. Flip now and cook till the other side is golden too.

Remove from pan and serve immediately with chutneys of your choice. I love it with it with Mint-Coriander Chutney! You can also fill Cheelas with fresh grated paneer!

MUTTER MUSHROOM KI SUBZI

Total: 25 mins
Prep: 10 mins
Cook: 15 mins
Yield: 4 Portions (4 Servings)

Ingredients
1 cup green peas (fresh or frozen)
About 1 pound/500 g. button mushrooms (cleaned and cut into □uarters)
1 large onion (chopped finely)
2 cloves garlic (chopped finely)
1/2 tsp. turmeric powder
1/2 tsp. cumin seeds
1/2 tsp. red chili powder
2 tbsp. vegetable cooking oil (or canola or sunflower oil)
Garnish: coriander (fresh, chopped)

Steps to Make It
Heat the cooking oil in a deep pan, on a medium flame. When hot, add the cumin seeds and fry till spluttering stops.
Add the garlic and fry till pale golden. Now add the onions and fry till soft.
Add the peas and mushrooms and the powdered spices. Add salt to taste and cook till the mushrooms begin to give off their juices. Stir occasionally. Turn off the fire.
Garnish with chopped coriander and serve with hot Chapatis (Indian flatbread) or Parathas (pan-fried Indian flatbread).

BESAN KA LADDOO (GRAM FLOUR SWEET)

Total: 40 mins
Prep: 20 mins
Cook: 20 mins
Yield: 4 Portions (4 Servings)

Ingredients
4 cups besan (Bengal gram flour)
2 cups ghee (clarified butter)
2 cups powdered sugar
1 tbsp. cardamom powder

Steps to Make It
Melt the ghee over a medium flame, in a thick-bottomed pan.
Add the besan and brown till you get a cooked aroma from it. The besan will also turn darker as it cooks and when done should be a deep golden brown color. This browning process can take up roughly 20 minutes.
Add the cardamom and mix well.
Turn off the fire and mix in the powdered sugar. Stir well.
Allow the mix to cool.
When cool, form into golf ball-sized rounds. Place on a lightly greased, flat tray till they set well.
Store in an air-tight container in a cool place.

A SHAHI TUKRA RECIPE

Total: 75 mins
Prep: 75 mins
Cook: 0 mins
Yield: One tray (6 servings)

Ingredients
4-1/2 cups (1 liter) of cream
1 can or about 1-3/4 cups (400 grams) sweetened condensed milk
1 teaspoon cardamom
Six to eight slices of raisin toast/bread
1/2 cup raisins/sultanasGhee for deep frying
1/4 cup blanched almond slivers (to garnish)

Steps to Make It
Mix the milk and condensed milk in a thick-bottomed pan and boil it until it reduces to half its original volume. Stir fre□uently to prevent from burning the milk.
When it is done add the cardamom, mix well and remove from the heat.
Cut the crusts off from the slices of bread/raisin toast and quarter the slices.
Heat the ghee on a medium flame. Deep fry the pieces of bread in it till they are crisp and golden. Drain them on paper towels.
In the same ghee, sauté the raisins till they puff up. Remove from the ghee and drain well on paper towels.

Put a layer of bread pieces at the bottom of a flat serving dish and top them with the thickened milk mixture. Keep adding layers of bread and the milk mixture alternating as you go, till all the bread and milk mixture is used up.

Garnish the dish with the raisins and almond slivers, chill for an hour and serve.

MARG MAKHANI: INDIAN BUTTER CHICKEN

Total: 105 mins
Prep: 60 mins
Cook: 45 mins
Yield: 6 servings

Ingredients
For the First Marinade
2 1/4 pounds boneless chicken (skin removed)
1 lime (or lemon, juiced)
Salt (to taste)
1 teaspoon red chili powder (adjust to suit your taste)
For the Second Marinade
1 cup fresh unsweetened yogurt (must not be sour)
2 teaspoons ground coriander
1 teaspoon ground cumin
1/4 teaspoon ground turmeric

For Cooking
3 tablespoons vegetable oil (or canola or sunflower cooking oil)
2 onions (chopped finely)
2 teaspoons garlic paste
1 teaspoon ginger paste
1 (14-ounce) can chopped tomatoes (ground into a smooth paste in a food processor)

2 cups chicken stock
2 tablespoons kasuri methi (dried fenugreek leaves)
3 tablespoons butter
Garnish: coriander (cilantro) leaves

For the Spice Powder
6 cloves
8 to 10 peppercorns
1-inch stick cinnamon
2 bay leaves
8 to 10 almonds
Seeds from 3 to 4 pods cardamom

Steps to Make It
Marinate the Chicken for the First Time
Mix the chicken, lime juice, salt, and red chili powder in a large, nonmetallic bowl.
Cover and allow to marinate for 1 hour.

Make the Spice Powder
Heat a flat pan or griddle over medium heat and gently roast (stirring freQuently) the cloves, peppercorns, cinnamon, bay leaves, and almonds until they darken slightly. Cool and add the cardamom seeds.
Now grind into a coarse powder in a clean, dry coffee grinder.

Marinate the Chicken for the Second Time
Mix the yogurt, spice powder (from the previous step), ground coriander, cumin, and turmeric and add them to the marinated chicken.
Cover and allow to marinate for 1 more hour.

Cook the Chicken
Heat the oil in a deep pan over medium heat. When hot, add the onions. Fry until pale golden brown in color and then add the ginger and garlic pastes. Fry for another minute.
Add the chicken (reserving the marinade) and fry until chicken turns opaQue and the flesh goes from pink to whitish in color.
Now add the ground tomatoes, chicken stock, kasuri methi, and the reserved yogurt-spice marinade to the chicken.
Cook until the chicken is tender and the gravy is reduced to half its original volume.
Melt the butter in another small pan and then pour it over the chicken.
Garnish with coriander leaves and serve with naan and kaali daal.

INDIAN TANDOORI CHICKEN

Total: 18 hrs 15 mins
Prep: 18 hrs
Cook: 15 mins
Yield: 4 to 6 servings

Ingredients
2 1/2 lbs. chicken (pieces of your choice with skin removed)
6 tbsp. tandoori masala
1 cup yogurt
1 tsp. garlic paste
Salt (to taste)
1 cup vegetable oil (or canola/sunflower cooking oil)
Garnish: 1 tbsp. chaat masala (available at most Indian grocers)
Garnish: onion rings

Steps to Make It
Gather the ingredients.
Make shallow diagonal slashes in the chicken pieces and keep aside.
Mix the tandoori masala with the yogurt, 2 tbsp. cooking oil, garlic paste and salt to taste to make a smooth paste.
Smear this paste all over the chicken pieces, ensuring you rub it well into the slashes you made earlier and that the pieces are well coated.

Put all the pieces and marinade into a deep bowl and cover. Refrigerate and allow to marinate for 12 to 18 hours.

Preheat your grill to medium. Put the chicken on it and □uickly sear (sealing in juices) on both sides. Now allow to brown on both sides, brushing cooking oil on as necessary.

Once browned, reduce heat and cover the grill. Cook till the chicken is tender. (Do not overcook or the chicken will dry out.)

When done, place chicken on a plate or platter and sprinkle chaat masala, garnish with lime juice, lime wedges and onion rings. Serve piping hot.

Enjoy!

Additional Option: Bake the Tandoori Chicken

Preheat your oven to 350 F/180 C.

While the oven is heating, line a baking tray with foil and spray the foil with cooking spray or smear with cooking oil. Lay the pieces on this foil and drizzle lightly with cooking oil.

Bake for approximately 15 minutes and then turn pieces and bake for another 10 minutes. Test chicken to see if cooked.

GRILLED CHICKEN TIKKA

Total: 12 hrs 15 mins
Prep: 12 hrs
Cook: 15 mins
Yield: 4-6 portions (4-6 servings)

Ingredients
1 cup fresh coriander (cilantro) leaves (finely chopped)
2 tbsp. ginger paste
3 tbsp. garlic paste
3 to 4 tbsp. garam masala
6 peppercorns (or 2 dry red chilies)
1/2 tsp. orange food coloring
1 cup fresh unsweetened yogurt (should not be sour)
2 1/4 lbs./1 kg. skinless and boneless chicken breast (or thigh, cut into 2-inch chunks)
1 large onion (cut into very thin rings)
3 tbsp. lime juice (or lemon juice, freshly squeezed)
Garnish: lime or lemon wedges
1 tsp. chaat masala (available at most Indian groceries)

Steps to Make It
Gather the ingredients.

Grind the chopped coriander (keep some aside for garnishing) and all other marinade ingredients (except yogurt) into a smooth paste in a food processor.

Pour the spice mix into a large bowl and add yogurt. Mix well. Add the chicken pieces and mix well. Cover the bowl and refrigerate. Allow to marinate overnight.

Thread the chicken onto skewers and keep ready.

Preheat your oven to 400 F or grill to medium-high.

Place the skewers on the grill or in your oven with a tray underneath to catch drippings. Roast open until the chicken is browned on all sides and tender, about 12 to 15 minutes. Remove from skewers and put the chicken on a plate.

Put the onion rings in a separate bowl and squeeze lime juice over them. Sprinkle the chaat masala over and mix well so the onions are fully coated. Garnish the chicken tikka with these onion rings and serve with naan.

Enjoy!

CHICKEN TIKKA MASALA RECIPE

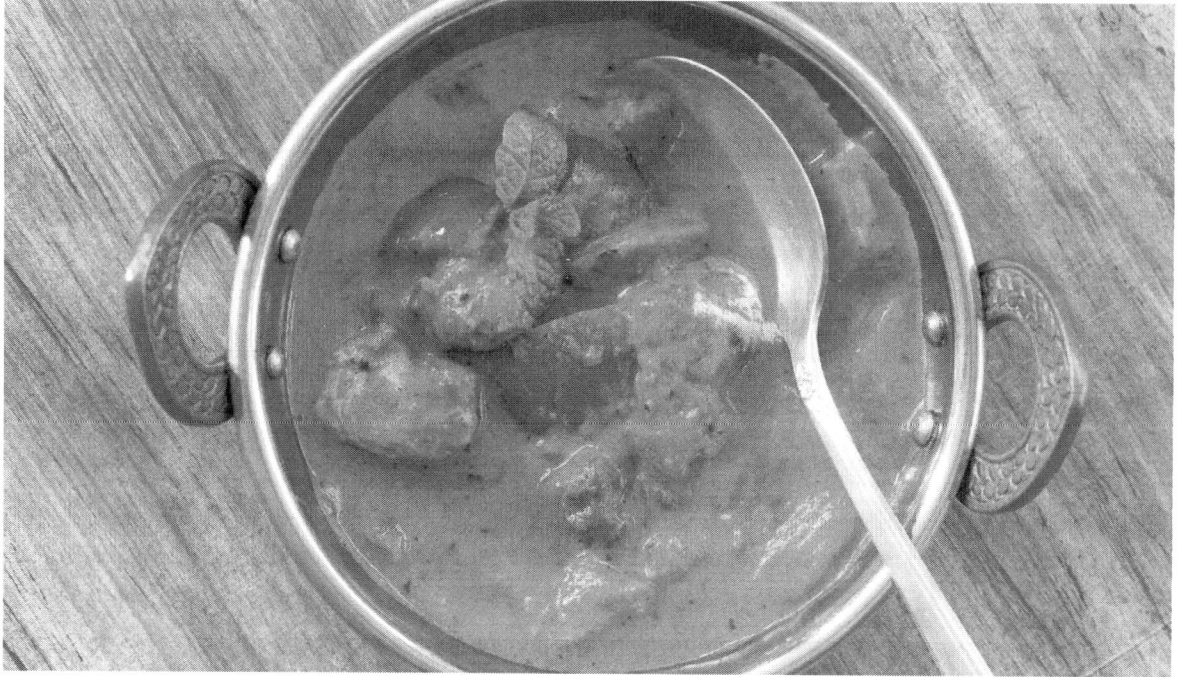

Total: 13 hrs 30 mins
Prep: 12 hrs
Cook: 90 mins
Yield: Serves 4

Ingredients
For the chicken marinade:
1 cup fresh yogurt (should not be sour)
1 cup finely chopped fresh coriander leaves ·
2 tbsps ginger paste
3 tbsps garlic paste
3 to 4 tbsps garam masala
6 peppercorns/ 2 dry red chilies
3 tbsps lime/ lemon juice
1/2 tsp orange food coloring
1 kg chicken (breast or thigh) skinless and cut into 2" chunks

For the gravy:
2 medium-sized onions finely chopped
6 cloves garlic chopped fine
5 pods cardamom
1 tin (400 gms approx) chopped tomatoes or 6 medium-sized fresh tomatoes chopped fine
2 tbsps garam masala

2 tsps soft brown sugar
1 cup single cream
3 tbsps almonds blanched and ground to a paste
3 tbsps vegetable/ canola/ sunflower cooking oil
Salt to taste

Steps to Make It

Grind the chopped coriander (keep some aside for garnishing) and all other marinade ingredients (except yogurt) to a smooth paste in a food processor.

Pour the above mix into a large bowl and add yogurt. Mix well. Add the chicken pieces and mix well. Cover the bowl and refrigerate. Allow to marinate overnight.

Thread the chicken onto skewers and keep ready.

Preheat your oven or grill to medium-high (200 C/400 F/Gas Mark 6). Place the skewers on the grill racks in your oven with a tray underneath to catch drippings. Roast open till the chicken is browned on all sides and tender. Keep aside.

Heat the oil in a deep pan on a medium flame and add the onion. Cook till soft.

Now add the cardamom and the garlic. Fry for 2 to 3 minutes.

Add the garam masala, brown sugar, tomatoes, almonds and mix well. Cook till the tomatoes are soft and a thick paste forms.

Add the grilled Chicken Tikka (chunks/ pieces) and stir. Cook for 10 minutes.

Add the cream and mix well. Turn off the flame. Garnish the dish with chopped coriander leaves and serve hot with Naans.

□

CHETTINAD CHICKEN CURRY

Total: 35 mins
Prep: 15 mins
Cook: 20 mins
Yield: 3-4 portions (3-4 servings)

Ingredients
1 tablespoon poppy seeds
1 teaspoon coriander seeds
1 teaspoon cumin seeds
1 teaspoon anise seed/fennel seeds
3 red chilies (dry)
1 stick cinnamon (1 inch)
2 cardamom pods
3 cloves
1/2 cup coconut (grated)
2 teaspoons ginger paste
2 teaspoons garlic paste
2 to 3 tablespoons vegetable oil (or sunflower, canola, or ghee)
10 to 15 curry leaves
2 large onions (sliced fine)

1 star anise
2 tomatoes (chopped fine)
Optional: 1 teaspoon chili powder
1-kilogram chicken (you can use a whole chicken cut into bits or leg or breast pieces)
Salt (to taste)
2 teaspoons lime juice
Garnish: chopped coriander leaves

Steps to Make It
Heat a heavy pan or skillet on a medium flame and roast the poppy, coriander, cumin and fennel seeds, dry red chilies, cinnamon, cardamom, cloves and coconut for 3 to 4 minutes. Remove from flame and allow to cool. Grind the mixture into a coarse powder in a clean, dry coffee grinder.
Mix the ginger and garlic pastes with this powder and keep aside.
In another deep pan, heat the oil and add the curry leaves. When they stop spluttering, add the sliced onions and fry till they are light brown.
Add the spice paste and star anise and fry for another 2 to 3 minutes.
Add the tomatoes and chili powder and stir well to mix all the ingredients.
Add the chicken, cover and simmer till it is tender.
When the chicken is done add lime juice, mix well and turn off the flame.
Garnish with coriander leaves and serve.
☐

BASIC CHICKEN CURRY

Total: 40 mins
Prep: 10 mins
Cook: 30 mins
Yield: 4 to 6 servings

Ingredients
1/4 cup vegetable, canola or sunflower oil
2 large onions (sliced thin)
2 large tomatoes (diced)
2 tbsp. garlic paste
1 tbsp. ginger paste
2 tsp. coriander powder
1 tsp. cumin powder
1/2 tsp. turmeric powder

1/2 tsp. red chili powder

2 tsp. garam masala powder

2 1/4 lb. (1 kg.) chicken pieces of your choice (skin removed)

1 1/2 cups hot water

Garnish: Chopped fresh coriander (cilantro)

Steps to Make It

Gather the ingredients.

Heat the oil in a deep skillet over medium heat and fry the onions until golden brown. Remove from the oil with a slotted spoon and drain on paper towels. Turn off heat, keeping oil in the pan.

Grind the onions into a smooth paste in a food processor. Remove to a bowl and set aside.

In the food processor, grind the tomatoes and garlic and ginger pastes together into a smooth paste.

Heat the oil in the skillet again and add the onion paste. Fry for 2 to 3 minutes. Add the tomato paste and all the spices. Mix well. (This is called masala.)

Fry the masala until the oil begins to separate from it.

Add the chicken to the masala and brown well, about 8 minutes.

Add 1 1/2 cups of hot water to the chicken, simmer, and cover. Cook until the chicken is tender, about 15 minutes.

Garnish with chopped coriander and serve with hot chapatis (Indian flatbread), Naans (tandoor-baked Indian flatbread) or plain boiled rice.

Serve and enjoy!

☐

MUGHLAI CHICKEN WITH GRAVY RECIPE

Total: 35 mins
Prep: 5 mins
Cook: 30 mins
Yield: 4-6 portions (4-6 servings)

Ingredients
10 to 15 almonds (blanched and skin removed)
1/4 cup ghee
2 onions (chopped finely)
1 tsp. ginger paste
2 tsp. garlic paste
1-inch stick of cinnamon
5 pods of cardamom
1 tsp. coriander powder
1 tsp. cumin powder
1 tsp. red chili powder
2 1/4 lbs. (1 kg.) boneless chicken (skin removed)
1 cup chicken stock
Salt (to taste)
5 to 6 tbsp. heavy cream (whisked)
2 tsp. garam masala

Steps to Make It

Grind the almonds into a fine paste and set aside.

Heat the ghee in a pan and fry the onions until they are translucent.

Add the ginger and garlic pastes, cinnamon and cardamom and fry for a minute.

Add coriander, cumin, and red chili powders and fry until the ghee begins to separate from the masala (the spice-onion mix). Add the chicken and fry until seared and chicken turns opa☐ue.

Add the stock and salt to taste and cook until the chicken is cooked through, about 10 to 15 minutes.

Whisk the cream to ensure that there are no lumps in it and add along with the almond paste to the chicken and stir well.

Turn off the heat and sprinkle the garam masala over the chicken. Cover the dish immediately.

You can either discard the cinnamon stick or use as a garnish. Serve after a few minutes with naan (Indian flatbread made in a tandoor or oven).

CHICKEN DHANSAK PARSI

Total: 100 mins
Prep: 10 mins
Cook: 90 mins
Yield: Serves 4

Ingredients
1 cup mixed lentils - toor, masoor, urad and moong (1/4 cup each)
1-liter chicken stock
500 grams of chicken pieces of your choice - boneless
10 black peppercorns
8 cloves
1-inch piece cinnamon
1/4 teaspoon grated nutmeg
1-inch piece of mace
2 large bay leaves
1 star anise
3 dry red chilies
1 tablespoon cumin seeds
1 tablespoon coriander seeds
1/2 teaspoon fenugreek seeds
1 teaspoon sesame seeds
1 teaspoon turmeric powder
1 large bunch each of fresh coriander leaves and fenugreek leaves (approximately 150 grams/ 0.33 pounds each)
1/2 bunch mint leaves (approximately 75 grams)
1 tablespoon tamarind paste

1 tablespoon garlic paste
1 tablespoon ginger paste
2 tablespoons vegetable/ canola/ sunflower cooking oil
Salt to taste

Steps to Make It

Wash the lentils well. Put them in a deep pan, add the chicken stock, salt to taste, and add a cup of water.

Boil until the lentils are soft. Add more water if re□uired.

While the lentils are boiling, heat a griddle or heavy-bottomed flat pan on a medium flame and dry roast all the spices (except the turmeric and nutmeg) until they begin to release their aroma.

Remove from the fire, cool, and then grind to a fine powder in a dry coffee or spice grinder. Mix in the turmeric and nutmeg and blend well. Set aside.

When the lentils are cooked soft, whisk them to get a smooth and thick soup-like consistency. Set aside.

Heat the cooking oil in a pan on a medium flame and when hot, add the fresh coriander, fenugreek, and mint leaves.

Fry till soft. Remove from the fire and cool. Grind into a smooth paste in a food processor.

Heat a deep, heavy-bottomed pan on a medium flame and add the lentils, ginger, garlic, and tamarind pastes and bring to a boil, stirring frequently to prevent sticking. The consistency should always be like a medium-thick soup.

Add a cup of water, the spice powder, coriander-fenugreek-mint paste you made earlier, salt if required, and the chicken pieces. Mix well.

Simmer and cook till chicken is done. Add more water to maintain consistency.

Serve Dhansak hot with Parsi brown rice and a Kachumbar salad.

GOAN-STYLE CHICKEN CAFREAL

Total: 50 mins
Prep: 30 mins
Cook: 20 mins
Rest Time: 10 hrs
Yield: 6 servings

Ingredients
1 whole chicken (butterflied)
2 tablespoons lemon juice (fresh from 1 large lemon, or use lime juice)
2 teaspoons salt (kosher)
6 red chilies (dry)
3 green chilies
6 peppercorns
30 cloves garlic
1 piece ginger (thumb-sized)

Steps to Make It
Pat the chicken dry, inside and out, with paper towels.

Make a salt paste by mixing just enough citrus juice to moisten 2 teaspoons of salt. Rub it over the chicken. Pour the remainder of the juice over the chicken and allow it to sit at room temperature for 30 minutes.

While the chicken marinates, grind the remaining ingredients together into a thick paste.

Rub this paste all over the chicken, cover it loosely and allow it to marinate in the refrigerator for 8 to 10 hours.

Cut the chicken into pieces to suit your size preference.

Heat enough oil to cover the chicken pieces in a Dutch oven or deep heavy pot to 350 degrees. Lower chicken pieces gently into the hot oil, being careful not to crowd the pot or reduce the heat. Cook in batches if necessary.

Flip the chicken pieces periodically, cooking until the internal temperature reaches 165 F as measured with a meat thermometer. This can take from 12 to 18 minutes.

☐

MUGHLAI BIRYANI INDIAN RECIPE

Total: 2 hrs 20 mins
Prep: 20 mins
Cook: 2 hrs
Yield: 4-6 portions (4-6 servings)

Ingredients
2 pounds lamb (or chicken cut into 2-inch pieces; if using chicken, use breast or thigh fillet)
4 large onions (sliced thin)
2 teaspoons garlic paste
2 teaspoons ginger paste
1/2 cup almonds
6 tablespoons ghee (or vegetable, canola or sunflower cooking oil)
1-inch stick of cinnamon
5 cloves
3 pods cardamom
8 peppercorns
2 teaspoons coriander powder
1 1/2 teaspoons cumin powder
1 teaspoon garam masala
1 cup yogurt
1 lime (juiced)

1 cup chicken stock (or beef stock)
2 tablespoons coriander leaves
2 tablespoons mint leaves (finely chopped)
Salt (to taste)
2 cups basmati rice
1 cup hot water
Salt (to taste)
Optional: 3 drops of green food coloring

Steps to Make It
Gather the ingredients.
Put the almonds in a bowl of hot water (enough to cover them) and set aside for 10 minutes.
After 10 minutes, remove the skins from all the almonds by pressing each one between your thumb and forefinger. The almonds will slip out of their skins.
Mix the garlic and ginger pastes and the peeled almonds and grind the mixture into a smooth paste in a food processor.
Wash the rice in a sieve and add enough water to fully cover the rice—at least 4 inches over the surface of the rice. Add salt to taste.
Boil the rice until it is almost done. To determine when the rice has reached that stage, remove a few grains from the pot and press them between your thumb and forefinger. The rice should mostly mash but will have a firm, white core. Turn off the burner.
Strain the rice through a colander and set it aside.
Heat 3 tablespoons of oil in a pan and fry two of the onions until they are caramelized and golden brown. Drain and set the onions aside on paper towels.
Heat 3 tablespoons of oil in another pan and add the whole spices—cinnamon, cardamom, cloves, and peppercorns. Fry the mixture until the spices turn a little darker.
Add the two remaining onions and fry them until they are translucent.
Add the ginger-garlic-almond paste and fry for two to three minutes.
Add all the spice powders—coriander, cumin, and garam masala and mix well.
Fry the mixture until the oil begins to separate from the masala and then add the lamb or chicken. Continue frying until the meat is fully sealed; it will become opaque and lose its pink color.
Add the yogurt, lime juice, stock, coriander and mint leaves and salt to taste (if needed). Mix well.
Add the yogurt, lime juice, stock, coriander and mint leaves and salt
Cover the pot and allow the dish to cook until the meat is tender.
If you are using food coloring, divide the rice into three e☐ual portions and put each portion into a separate dish. Add the orange food coloring to one portion of the rice and the green food coloring to another portion. Leave the third portion white.
Add food coloring to different portions of rice
With each portion, mix the rice until all the grains are well colored.
Mix rice with food coloring
Set the rice aside for 10 minutes, and then mix the three portions in a bowl.
Mix portions of rice in bowl

Grease a deep baking dish and evenly layer the cooked rice and meat (and its gravy) to form at least two sets of layers—rice-meat-rice-meat-rice. Garnish with the previously caramelized onions.

Layer rice and meat in cooking dish

Cover the dish tightly. If the dish does not have a cover, use two layers of aluminum foil with the shiny side of both layers pointing down toward the rice, and secure the foil to the dish with baking string.

Cover dish with aluminum foil

Put the dish in a preheated oven set at 350 F. Bake for 20 minutes.

Turn off the oven and let the dish sit in the oven until you are ready to eat. Remove the foil only when you are ready to eat.

Serve and enjoy!□

BADAMI MURGH KORMA (INDIAN CHICKEN KORMA)

Total: 95 mins
Prep: 60 mins
Cook: 35 mins
Yield: serves 4 to 6

Ingredients
2 pounds skinless chicken thighs (cut into 2" pieces, bone-in or boneless)
1 cup fresh unsweetened yogurt
1/2 teaspoon turmeric powder
3 to 4 tablespoons vegetable/canola/sunflower oil
3 large onions (finely chopped)
2 teaspoons garlic paste
2 teaspoons ginger paste
2" cinnamon stick
6 cloves
10 peppercorns
2 pieces of mace
5 green cardamom pods (split)

2 teaspoons coriander powder
1 teaspoon cumin powder
1/2 teaspoon red chili powder
1/4 teaspoon nutmeg powder
4 tablespoons finely ground almond meal
Salt to taste
Approximately 2 tablespoons fresh green coriander (finely chopped)

Steps to Make It

Put the chicken, yogurt, salt to taste and turmeric powder into a deep mixing bowl. Stir to mix well and coat all the chicken completely. Keep aside to marinate for an hour.

When the chicken has marinated, heat the vegetable/canola/sunflower cooking oil in a deep, heavy-bottomed pan over medium heat. When hot, add the onions and fry till almost pale golden. Add the ginger and garlic pastes and fry for 1 minute. Stir often to prevent burning.

Add all the whole spices (cinnamon, cloves, peppercorns, mace and cardamom pods) and fry for 1 minute, or till spices are slightly darker in color.

Now, add all the powdered spices (coriander, cumin, red chili and nutmeg) and fry till the oil begins to separate from the masala (spice mix). Stir often to prevent burning. If required, sprinkle in a little water from time to time to prevent the masala from burning. Next, add the marinated chicken/yogurt/turmeric powder mixture and the almond meal and stir well. The gravy for this dish should be thick.

Cover and cook until the chicken is tender. If you find the dish is getting dry or the chicken or masala is sticking to the bottom of the pan, add 1/2 cup of warm water and stir gently and thoroughly. Once the chicken is cooked, if there is too much gravy, reduce it by removing the lid and continuing to cook.

When done, remove the pan from heat and put Korma into a serving dish.

Garnish with chopped fresh coriander. Serve piping hot with bread like Chapatis, Parathas or Naans (leavened flatbread made baked in a tandoor or oven).

Enjoy!

☐

TANDOORI PANEER TIKKA

Total: 2 hrs 45 mins
Prep: 2 hrs 20 mins
Cook: 25 mins
Yield: 4 servings

Ingredients
3 tablespoons tandoori masala (homemade or store-bought, divided)
1/4 cup yogurt
5 to 6 tablespoons vegetable oil (or canola or sunflower cooking oil, divided)
Kosher salt (to taste)
1/2 pound paneer (homemade or store-bought, cut into 30 (2-inch) cubes)
1 large onions (cut into 1-inch s☐uare pieces)
1 red bell pepper (deseeded and cut into 2-inch cubes)
1 green bell pepper (deseeded and cut into 2-inch cubes)
2 tablespoons chaat masala (available at Indian grocery stores)
Lemon juice (to taste)
Garnish: lemon wedges

Steps to Make It
Gather the ingredients.

Put the paneer chunks in a bowl and pour the tandoori paste over it. Mix gently to coat the paneer. Cover and marinate in the refrigerator for two hours.

Put paneer chunks in a bowl

Mix the remaining 1/2 tablespoon of tandoori masala with the onions to coat them well.

Pour mixture over onions

Thread the marinated paneer, onion, and green and red bell pepper pieces onto bamboo skewers.

Preheat your grill on medium.

Place the paneer skewers on the hot grill and brush with a little cooking oil.

Grill until the paneer is light golden and the onions are soft. Do not overcook, or the paneer will become rubbery.

Remove onto a plate and sprinkle with chaat masala.

Squeeze some lemon juice over the paneer skewers, garnish with lemon wedges, and serve hot.

Enjoy!

☐

INDIAN ROAST LEG OF LAMB (MASALA RAAN) RECIPE

Total: 31 hrs 30 mins
Prep: 28 hrs
Cook: 3 hrs 30 mins
Yield: 4 to 6 servings Indian lamb

Ingredients
For the Lamb:
4.4-pound (2 kg-) trimmed leg of lamb (see below for directions)
For the Marinade:
1 pound (1/2 kg) onions (cut into ⬜uarters)
1.77 ounces (50 g) almonds
3 green chilies
2 tablespoons garlic paste
1 tablespoon ginger paste
17.64 ounces (500 g) unsweetened yogurt
2 tablespoons cumin
3 tablespoon coriander
1/2 teaspoon red chili powder
1 teaspoon garam masala
Salt to taste

5 tablespoons neutral oil like vegetable, canola or sunflower
8 to 10 whole cloves
15 pods green cardamom
2 (1-inch) sticks cinnamon
12 to 15 black peppercorns

Steps to Make It
Prepare the Lamb
Trim all the fat off the leg of lamb. Using a sharp, pointed knife, remove any sinew (which looks like a thin, almost transparent film on parts of the meat).
Alternatively, have your butcher do this for you. If the leg will be too large for your pans or your oven, ask the butcher to cut it into two pieces.
Use a sharp knife to cut deep slashes all over the meat. This allows the marinade to penetrate the meat and makes for a seriously well-flavored leg of lamb.
Place the meat in the center of a well-greased baking dish or pan.

Marinate the Meat
Place the quartered onions, almonds, green chilies, and garlic and ginger pastes into a food processor and grind into a smooth, thick paste, only adding water while grinding if absolutely necessary.
In a separate bowl whisk the yogurt until smooth and then mix it with the paste you just made.
Add the cumin, coriander, red chili powder, and gram masala to the yogurt and mix to blend well.
Now add the onion-almond paste that you ground earlier. Mix everything until completely combined.
Pour this marinade all over the meat and use your hands to rub the marinade into the meat, pushing it into the slashes you cut on the surface of the leg. Make sure all of the meat is well covered with the marinade.
Cling wrap the baking dish and refrigerate for 24 hours.

Roast the Lamb
Remove the marinated leg of lamb from the refrigerator and keep out to warm up to room temperature.
Heat the oven to 400 F (200 C/Gas Mark 6).
When the leg of lamb has warmed up to room temperature, remove the cling film.
In a skillet, heat the oil and, when hot, add all the whole spices -- cloves, cardamom, cinnamon, and peppercorns. Sauté until they stop sizzling and begin to give off an aroma.
Pour the oil with the spices in it, all over the marinated meat. Now cover the pan tightly with foil.
Put the pan in the heated oven and cook for 2 hours.
Uncover the raan and cook for 1 more hour. Baste the raan every 10 minutes or so to ensure it remains moist.
Remove the raan from the oven and allow to rest for 20 minutes.

Carve the rested lamb into thick slices and serve garnished with the slivered almonds. You can spoon the pan juices over the meat if desired.

Masala raan goes well with plain rice and a salad or with Indian flatbreads known as parathas or naan.

INDIAN CHICKEN KABAB (MURG MALAI)

Total: 2 hrs 30 mins
Prep: 2 hrs
Cook: 30 mins
Yield: 1 pound (4 to 5 servings)

Ingredients
For the Chicken:
1 pound/500 g. chicken thighs (bones removed and cut into 2-inch cubes)

For the First Marinade:
1/2 teaspoon freshly ground white pepper
1/4 teaspoon cardamom
1 teaspoon salt (or to taste)
1 tablespoon garlic paste
2 teaspoons to 1 tablespoon ginger paste

For the Second Marinade:
1/2 cup grated mild cheddar cheese or mozzarella cheese
1/2 cup sour cream

Salt (to taste)
2 green chilies
1/2 cup fresh green coriander leaves
1 tablespoon neutral cooking oil like vegetable, canola or sunflower oil

To Serve:
Pinch
Chaat masala
1 lemon to garnish

Steps to Make It
Make the First Marinade
Pat the chicken cubes dry with paper towels to help the marinade adhere to it better. When this is done, lay the pieces out neatly in a flat dish.
Sprinkle the white pepper, cardamom and the first lot of salt over the chicken. Also, add the garlic and ginger pastes.
Mix thoroughly to ensure that the chicken is fully coated. Cover with plastic and put into the refrigerator to marinate for 30 minutes.
Make the Second Marinade
While the chicken is marinating, prepare the remaining part of the marinade. Put the grated cheese in a deep bowl and mash it with clean hands to ensure that it forms a paste and has no lumps.
Now add the sour cream and salt to taste to the cheese and continue to mash and mix so that there are no lumps in the mixture.
Grind the coriander leaves and green chilies into a coarse paste using a blender or a mortar and pestle. Add this coarse paste to the cheese-sour cream mixture and stir to blend well.
After the chicken has marinated in the first part of the marinade for 30 minutes, add it to the second part of the marinade—the cheese-sour cream-coriander chili mix. Combine well to ensure all the chicken pieces are well coated.
Now add the oil and mix well again. Allow the chicken to rest for 1 hour.
Assemble, Cook and Serve the Kababs
Heat your oven or barbecue grill to 450 F/230 C/Gas Mark 8.
Soak your bamboo skewers in water so that they don't burn during the cooking process.
When the chicken has marinated for 1 hour, thread 3 to 4 pieces on each skewer, ensuring that you do it in a way so as to expose most of the chicken to the heat.
When you have threaded all the chicken onto skewers, lay the skewers on a baking tray and put into your oven. Cook for 15 minutes, remove and turn the skewers so that the part of the chicken pieces that was facing down, is now facing up. Put back into the oven and cook for another 15 minutes.
When done, gently remove the chicken pieces from the skewers and arrange on a serving plate. You also can leave the skewers as is and serve as individual portions.
Garnish with a sprinkling of the chaat masala and a squeeze of lemon juice. Serve murg malai kabab with naan and a salad to make a meal or serve it just by itself as an appetizer.

GRILLED TANDOORI COD

Total: 27 mins
Prep: 8 mins
Cook: 19 mins
Yield: Serves 4

Ingredients
4-6 cod fillets
For the Marinade:
1 cup/240 milliliters plain yogurt
1/4 cup/60 milliliters olive oil
4 garlic cloves (minced)
2 teaspoons/10 milliliters ginger (fresh, grated)
2 teaspoons/10 milliliters cumin (ground)
2 teaspoons/10 milliliters coriander (ground)
1 teaspoon/5 milliliters red pepper (or mild chili powder)
1 teaspoon/5 milliliters turmeric
1 teaspoon/5 milliliters sea salt
For the Garnish:
1/2 onion (small red, cut into thin rings)
1/4 cup/60 milliliters cilantro (leaves)

Steps to Make It

Cut the cod fillets into pieces measuring 1 1/2 inch (or larger, if desired).

In a medium bowl, combine all the marinade ingredients: yogurt, olive oil, minced garlic, grated ginger, ground cumin, ground coriander, red pepper, turmeric, and sea salt.

Place the fish pieces in the marinade bowl, tossing them with the marinade to coat them well. Cover the bowl with plastic wrap and let it marinate in the refrigerator for 1 hour. Do not leave the fish and marinade out at room temperature.

Preheat the grill for medium-high heat. Place fish pieces in a grill wok and cook for about 9 minutes. When fish is opaque, toss fish with heat resistant utensils, and cook for an additional 5 to 7 minutes.

Remove the fish from the heat and serve topped with red onion slices and cilantro leaves.

While you can use ground cumin and coriander, you will boost the flavor and complexity tremendously if you buy whole cumin and coriander seeds and make your own freshly ground spices right before using them in the marinade. Simply toast the seeds in a skillet and grind them in a clean coffee grinder or with a mortar and pestle. You simply won't go back to pre-ground spices.

FISH MAKHANI - FISH IN CREAMY GRAVY

Total: 2 hrs 30 mins
Prep: 2 hrs
Cook: 30 mins
Yield: Serves 4 to 6 people

Ingredients
1 kg fish fillets (any fish with firm white flesh) skin removed, cut into 2' pieces
First, marinate the fish in:
Juice of 1 lime
Salt to taste
1 tsp red chili powder (adjust to suit your taste)

Then add:
6 cloves
8 to 10 peppercorns
1-inch stick of cinnamon
2 bay leaves
8 to 10 almonds
Seeds from 3 to 4 pods of cardamom
1 cup fresh yogurt (must not be sour)

For the gravy:
3 tbsps vegetable/canola/sunflower cooking oil
2 onions chopped

2 tsp garlic paste
1 tsp ginger paste
2 tsp coriander powder
1 tsp cumin powder
1/4 tsp turmeric powder .
400g/ 14-ounce of chopped tomatoes, half of them ground into a smooth paste in a food processor, the other half left whole
1/2 liter fish stock
2 tbsp kasuri methi (dried fenugreek leaves)
3 tbsps unmelted, soft butter
Salt to taste
Coriander leaves to garnish

Steps to Make It
Mix the fish, lime juice, salt and red chilli powder in a large, non-metallic bowl. Cover and allow to marinate for 1 hour.

Heat a flat pan or griddle on medium heat and gently roast (stirring frequently) the cloves, peppercorns, cinnamon, bay leaves and almonds till they darken slightly. Cool and add the cardamom seeds. Now grind into a coarse powder in a clean, dry coffee grinder.

Mix the yogurt, above whole spice powder, coriander, cumin, and turmeric powders together and add them to the fish. Allow it to marinate for another hour.

Heat the oil in a deep pan over medium heat. When hot, add the onions. Fry till a pale golden brown in color and then add the ginger and garlic pastes. Fry for a minute.

Add only the fish from the fish-spice mix and fry till sealed (fish will turn opa☐ue and the flesh will go from pink to whitish in color). Stir very gently.

Now add the tomato paste and chopped tomatoes, fish stock, kasuri methi and remaining part of the yogurt-spice mix to the fish.

Cook till the fish is tender and the gravy is reduced to half its original volume. Stir very gently every now and then to avoid breaking the fish up.

Melt the butter in another small pan and then pour it over the fish. Garnish with coriander leaves and serve with Naan, Kaali Daal, and a salad.

INDIAN-STYLE STUFFED ROAST CHICKEN

Total: 4 hrs 45 mins
Prep: 3 hrs 5 mins
Cook: 100 mins
Yield: 1 chicken (5 to 8 servings)

Ingredients
1 whole chicken (roughly 3.3 pounds/1.5 kg.)
3 tablespoons neutral oil (to drizzle on chicken when roasting)

For the Marinade:
2 tablespoons yogurt (unsweetened)
2 tablespoons lime juice (or lemon juice)
2 teaspoons garlic paste
1 teaspoon ginger paste
1/2 teaspoon red chili powder
1/2 teaspoon turmeric powder
1/2 teaspoon salt

For the Filling:
3 tablespoons neutral oil (vegetable/canola/sunflower)
3/4 teaspoon cumin seeds

2 medium onions (chopped fine)
2 teaspoons garlic paste
1 teaspoon ginger paste
10 ounces/300 g ground beef (or lamb)
1 tablespoon coriander (ground)
1 teaspoon cumin (ground)
1 tablespoon garam masala
Salt to taste
2 medium tomatoes (chopped fine)
1 cup fresh/frozen peas
1 large potato (peeled and cut into 1-inch cubes)
1 teaspoon lime juice (or lemon juice)
1/4 cup fresh coriander leaves (chopped)

Steps to Make It
Prepare the Chicken
Thoroughly wash the chicken inside, removing any organs or giblet packets, and outside. Pat dry with paper towels and set aside.
In a large, deep bowl, mix together yogurt, 2 tablespoons lime juice, 2 teaspoons garlic paste, 1 teaspoon ginger paste, chili powder, turmeric, and salt.
Place the whole chicken into this marinade and coat it well. Cover the dish with plastic wrap and marinate for 2 to 3 hours in the refrigerator.

Make the Filling
Heat 3 tablespoons oil in a wok or deep pan on medium heat.
Add the cumin seeds and fry for 1 minute. Add the onions and fry until they turn a pale golden color.
Add 2 teaspoons garlic paste and 1 teaspoon ginger paste and fry for 1 minute.
Add the ground meat, ground coriander, cumin, garam masala, and salt to taste.
Continue to brown the ground meat, stirring often to prevent burning. This should take about 5 to 7 minutes.
Add the tomatoes, peas, and potatoes and stir and cook until the potatoes are soft.
Turn the heat off and add the lime juice and chopped coriander leaves. Mix well.

Cook the Chicken
Preheat oven to 350 F/175 C/Gas Mark 4.
Remove the marinated chicken from the refrigerator and fill the stomach cavity with the minced meat stuffing. Try to get all the stuffing in if possible.
Put in a baking/roasting dish and drizzle all over with cooking oil.
Roast the chicken, uncovered for 1 hour and 15 minutes. It will, ideally, be golden in color by now and ready to eat.
Serve and enjoy!
☐

MURGH METHI MALAI RECIPE

Total: 55 mins
Prep: 10 mins
Cook: 45 mins
Yield: serves 4-6

Ingredients
1 kg of chicken pieces, skin removed and marinated with...
For the marinade: 12-15 cloves of garlic
3" piece of fresh ginger
8 whole dry red chillies
1 and a 1/2 tsp salt
1 and a 1/2 tsp of freshly ground black pepper powder
For spice masala powder: 2 tsps cumin seeds
3 tsps black pepper corns
2 star anise
2 X 1" sticks of cinnamon
6 green cardamoms
3 black cardamoms

12 cloves
A big pinch of grated nutmeg
2 tbsps coriander seeds
5 bay leaves
Other: 3 large onions, to be made into a coarse paste
3 tbsps vegetable/ canola/ sunflower cooking oil/ ghee
1 and a 1/2 cups of skimmed milk
5 tbsps heavy cream
3 tbsps of dried Kasoori methi (or a cup of fresh fenugreek leaves chopped coarsely)
Salt to taste

Steps to Make It
Gather the ingredients.
Use a food processor to make a fine paste of the ginger, garlic and the dry red chillies.
When the paste is ready, add the salt and pepper. Mix it into the chicken pieces and keep aside in the fridge to marinate for 3 to 4 hours.
Now to make the dry masala powder: Roast the coriander seeds and the bay leaves lightly and grind to powder.
Make a powder of the remaining spices without roasting and keep aside.
Heat a non-stick flat bottomed pan on medium heat. When hot, pour in the onion paste to roast it lightly, adding a bit of salt gets the onion to cook sooner and it gets caramelized easily.
When the onion paste gets a little browned, add in the marinade and chicken, stir and cook on medium heat till the chicken and masala paste mixture starts releasing its own fat.
Now add the ghee/ vegetable/ canola/ sunflower oil. Stir to mix well.
Next, add the powdered spices and keep sautéing for 3-5 more minutes.
Reduce heat a little, cover and cook for about 10 minutes, or till the chicken is done.
Next, pour in the milk, adjust the seasoning according to taste and bring the pot to a boil.
Next, pour in the cream and follow with crushed kasoori methi.
Mix well, cover and cook for another 3 to 4 minutes till the aroma of the fenugreek is absorbed into the gravy.
Serve hot with freshly made Naan or Chapatis.
☐

CHICKEN TIKKA MASALA RECIPE

Total: 13 hrs 30 mins
Prep: 12 hrs
Cook: 90 mins
Yield: Serves 4

Ingredients
For the chicken marinade:
1 cup fresh yogurt (should not be sour)
1 cup finely chopped fresh coriander leaves
2 tbsps ginger paste
3 tbsps garlic paste
3 to 4 tbsps garam masala
6 peppercorns/ 2 dry red chilies
3 tbsps lime/ lemon juice
1/2 tsp orange food coloring
1 kg chicken (breast or thigh) skinless and cut into 2" chunks

For the gravy:
2 medium-sized onions finely chopped
6 cloves garlic chopped fine

5 pods cardamom
1 tin (400 gms approx) chopped tomatoes or 6 medium-sized fresh tomatoes chopped fine
2 tbsps garam masala
2 tsps soft brown sugar
1 cup single cream
3 tbsps almonds blanched and ground to a paste
3 tbsps vegetable/ canola/ sunflower cooking oil
Salt to taste

Steps to Make It

Grind the chopped coriander (keep some aside for garnishing) and all other marinade ingredients (except yogurt) to a smooth paste in a food processor.

Pour the above mix into a large bowl and add yogurt. Mix well. Add the chicken pieces and mix well. Cover the bowl and refrigerate. Allow to marinate overnight.

Thread the chicken onto skewers and keep ready.

Preheat your oven or grill to medium-high (200 C/400 F/Gas Mark 6). Place the skewers on the grill racks in your oven with a tray underneath to catch drippings. Roast open till the chicken is browned on all sides and tender. Keep aside.

Heat the oil in a deep pan on a medium flame and add the onion. Cook till soft.

Now add the cardamom and the garlic. Fry for 2 to 3 minutes.

Add the garam masala, brown sugar, tomatoes, almonds and mix well. Cook till the tomatoes are soft and a thick paste forms.

Add the grilled Chicken Tikka (chunks/ pieces) and stir. Cook for 10 minutes.

Add the cream and mix well. Turn off the flame. Garnish the dish with chopped coriander leaves and serve hot with Naans.

INDIAN LAMB DISH

Total: 70 mins
Prep: 30 mins
Cook: 40 mins
Yield: 4 Servings

Ingredients
2 to 2 1/2 pounds lamb (cubed)
1/2 cup yogurt
4 tablespoons vegetable oil (or canola or sunflower cooking oil)
1 (2-inch) stick cinnamon
5 to 6 cardamom pods
8 to 10 cloves
2 bay leaves
1 teaspoon peppercorns
2 medium-sized onions (finely chopped)
2 tablespoons ginger paste
2 teaspoon coriander powder
1 teaspoon cumin powder

1/4 teaspoon turmeric powder
3 to 4 Kashmiri dry red chilies (coarsely ground)
2 teaspoon garam masala
2 cups beef stock (or lamb stock)
1 cup of water
Kosher salt (to taste)
5 teaspoons light cream (or half-and-half)
Garnish: coriander leaves

Steps to Make It
Gather the ingredients.
In a bowl, mix the lamb and yogurt and keep aside. This will tenderize the lamb.
Heat the oil in a deep pan and add the cinnamon, cardamom, cloves, bay leaves, and peppercorns. Fry till they turn slightly darker in color.
Now add the onions and fry until they turn light golden.
Add the ginger and garlic paste and fry for a minute.
Add the coriander, cumin, turmeric, Kashmiri chilies, and garam masala and fry until the oil separates from the masala.
Add the meat and yogurt mix to the masala and fry well.
Add the beef stock, water, and salt, to taste.
Cook till the gravy is reduced. Stir often. The gravy should be thick when done.
Whisk the cream until smooth.
Stir it into the curry to mix well.
Garnish with coriander leaves and serve with plain boiled rice or pulao and a vegetable side dish.
Enjoy!

☐

INDIAN VEGGIE BALLS (MALAI KOFTA)

Ingredients
For the Koftas
2 cups potatoes (peeled and diced)
1 cup mixed vegetables (carrots, beans, peas, sweet corn; boiled)
1 cup paneer cubes
2 tablespoons heavy cream
1 teaspoon cumin powder
1 teaspoon coriander powder
1/2 teaspoon red chili powder
Salt (to taste)
1/2 cup chopped nuts (almonds, walnuts, and cashew nuts)
1/4 cup of raisins (finely chopped)
3 cups vegetable (or canola or sunflower cooking oil for frying, or more as needed)

For the Sauce
3 tablespoons vegetable oil (or canola or sunflower cooking oil)

2 large onions (quartered)
2 tomatoes (□uartered)
2 tablespoons garlic paste
1 tablespoon ginger paste
2 teaspoons coriander powder
1 tablespoon cumin powder
1/2 teaspoon red chili powder
1 teaspoon poppy seeds (lightly roasted and ground into a powder)
3 tablespoons nuts (cashews and almonds, ground into a thick paste)
1 cup water (warm)
Salt (to taste)
2 teaspoon garam masala

Steps to Make It
Note: while there are multiple steps to this recipe, this kofta dish is broken down into workable categories to help you better plan for preparation and baking.
Making the Koftas
Wash, peel, and dice the potatoes.
Wash and peel potatoes
Boil them in a pot of water until fork tender.
Boil potatoes
Drain and set aside.
Next, boil the veggies until crisp-tender.
Drain and set aside.
In a large bowl, mash the boiled potatoes, mixed vegetables, paneer, and cream together.
Add the kofta spices - cumin, coriander, and red chili powder - to this mash and mix well. The resulting dough should be firm. If not add some more boiled potato. Season with salt.
In a small bowl, combine the chopped nuts and raisins.
Make this dough into balls and put a 1/2 teaspoon of the nut and raisin mix in the center of each ball.
Roll into perfect rounds.
In a large pot, heat the oil kept aside to fry the koftas, on a medium flame.
Deep fry these rounds till pale golden in color.
Drain on paper towels and keep aside.
Lay out of paper towels

Make the Sauce
Heat the 3 tablespoons of oil in a deep pan and fry the onions till light brown.
In a small food processor, place the fried onions, tomatoes, ginger, garlic, coriander, cumin, and red chili powder, and grind into a paste.

NAVRATAN KORMA - NINE-GEM CURRY

Total: 35 mins
Prep: 10 mins
Cook: 25 mins
Yield: 4-6 servings

Ingredients
4 tbsps vegetable/ canola/ sunflower cooking oil
1/2 cup cashews, broken into bits
1 cup paneer (cottage cheese) cubes (1" cubes) - see recipe below
2 medium-sized onions chopped and ground to a fine paste
2 tsps garlic paste
1 tsp ginger paste
3 tomatoes chopped and ground to a fine paste
1 tsp coriander powder
1/2 tsp cumin powder
1/2 tsp turmeric powder
1/2 tsp red chilli powder
1 tsp garam masala powder
1 cup peeled, cubed, parboiled potato
12-15 french beans, tops and tails removed, parboiled
2 medium carrots chopped into small cubes and parboiled

1/2 cup green peas, parboiled
1 cup cauliflower florets, parboiled
1 medium-sized green bell pepper, seeds removed and cut into 1" squares
1 cup pineapple cubes
3 tbsps thickened/ double/ heavy cream
Salt to taste

Steps to Make It
Gather the ingredients.
Heat a deep pan on medium flame and add 1 tsp of cooking oil to it. Now add the cashews and fry till slightly darker. Remove with a slotted spoon and keep aside on paper towels, for later use.
Do the same for the paneer cubes and keep aside for later.
In the same pan, add the remaining cooking oil and heat. Now add the onion paste and fry till slightly browned.
Add the garlic and ginger pastes and fry for 1 minute. Now add the tomato paste and fry for another 1 minute.
Add all the spice powders and fry the masala till the oil begins to separate from it. Stir often to keep the masala from sticking to the pan and burning.
Now add 1 cup of warm water to this masala and mix well. Cook for 1 minute.
Add all the vegetables, pineapple, paneer and previously fried cashews. Mix gently but well making sure not to mash or break the pieces of the vegetable. Cook till veggies are done but not limp (they must be al dente!)
Add the cream, season with salt to taste, stir and turn off heat.
Serve with hot Naans (leavened, tandoor-baked Indian flatbread).
☐

PUNJABI SARSON KA SAAG (GREENS AND SPICES)

Total: 30 mins
Prep: 10 mins
Cook: 20 mins
Yield: 2 to 4 servings

Ingredients
1 bunch (1/2 pound) spinach (washed and finely chopped)
1 bunch (1/2 pound) mustard greens (washed and finely chopped)
2 green chilies
Dash of salt, or to taste
2 to 3 tablespoons ghee (clarified butter)
1 large onion (grated)
1 tablespoon grated ginger or ginger paste
1 tablespoon grated garlic or garlic paste
1 teaspoon coriander
1 teaspoon cumin
1 teaspoon garam masala
1 tablespoon lime juice (juice of 1/2 a lime or lemon)
1 tablespoon Bengal gram flour or maize flour
Garnish: Unsalted butter

Steps to Make It

Gather the ingredients.

In a medium pot, mix the spinach, mustard greens, green chilies, and salt to taste. Add 1 cup water and boil until cooked.

Mash the greens and mix well to make a coarse paste.

In another pan, heat the ghee on a medium flame. When hot, add the grated onion and fry until a pale golden color.

Add the remaining ingredients and fry until the oil separates from the masala (onion-spice mix).

Add the greens to this and stir until fully blended.

Garnish with a dollop of butter and serve with makki ki roti (Indian maize flatbread).

Enjoy!

☐

INDIAN BLACK LENTILS (KAALI DAAL)

Total: 75 mins
Prep: 15 mins
Cook: 60 mins
Yield: 4 portions (4 servings)

Ingredients
1 cup split urad daal (black lentils, soaked overnight in water to cover)
3 cups water
2 large onions (sliced thin)
2 green chilies (slit)
Pinch of asafetida
Salt (to taste)
2 tablespoons neutral oil (like vegetable, canola or sunflower)
2-inch piece of ginger (julienned)
1 tablespoon garlic (minced)
2 large tomatoes (chopped into cubes)
2 teaspoons coriander
1 teaspoon ground cumin
1/2 teaspoon red chili powder
1/2 cup heavy cream (whisked)

2 tablespoons ghee
1 teaspoon cumin seeds

Steps to Make It
Soak the urad daal (black lentils) in a bowl of water overnight.
Boil the soaked lentils with 3 cups of water, 1 sliced onion, green chilies, asafetida, and salt to taste till they are very tender. Set aside.
In a separate pan, heat the oil and fry the other onion until soft. Add the ginger and garlic and fry for 1 minute.
Add the tomatoes, coriander, cumin, and red chili powder and fry for another 5 minutes.
Add the reserved boiled lentils and enough water to make a thick gravy-like consistency and mix well. Simmer for 10 minutes.
Pour in the whisked cream and mix well. Turn off the fire.
In another small pan, heat the ghee and when hot add the cumin seeds and cook till they stop spluttering.
Pour this into the lentils (it will all sizzle) and mix well.
Serve hot with a vegetable side dish and naans (tandoor-baked leavened Indian flatbread) or butter chicken and naan.
☐

INDIAN PAPDI CHAAT

Total: 35 mins
Prep: 15 mins
Cook: 20 mins
Yield: Up to 4 servings

Ingredients
For the Papdi Dough
1 cup all-purpose flour
4 tablespoons ghee
1 teaspoon onion seeds
Kosher salt (to taste)
Water (enough to create dough)
Vegetable oil (or canola or sunflower cooking oil, to deep fry)
For the Toppings
5 large potatoes
1 cup chickpeas
Kosher salt (to taste)
For Assembly and Serving

2 cups fresh yogurt (whisked till smooth and chilled)
2 red onions (very finely chopped)
2 large tomatoes (very finely chopped)
1 cup tamarind chutney
1 cup mint-coriander chutney
2 cups fine sev (or gram flour)
2 teaspoons red chili powder
2 tablespoons cumin seeds (gently roasted and powdered)
3 teaspoons powdered black rock salt
Garnish: 1/4 cup fresh coriander leaves (finely chopped)

Steps to Make It
Note: while there are multiple steps to this recipe, this papdi dish is broken down into workable categories to help you better plan for preparation and cooking.

Make the Papdi Dough
Mix the flour, ghee, onion seeds, and salt, to taste, and mix well.
Add just a little water at a time and knead to get a firm, smooth dough.
Cover it with a damp cloth and allow it to rest for 20 minutes.
After the dough has rested, divide it into equal-sized balls. Roll the dough balls between your palms till smooth.
Lightly flour a clean rolling surface and press one ball flat.
Roll the dough balls out into a 1/4-inch thick circle using a rolling pin.
Use the circular cookie cutter to cut smaller circles out on the large circle. Remove extra dough from sides of smaller circles. Keep them on a lightly floured tray or plate for later frying (they will become the papdis).
Repeat till all the dough is used up.
Heat oil for deep frying in a deep pan on a medium flame.
When it is hot, add the papdis a few at a time and fry till they are crisp and pale golden.
Drain and keep the cooked dough on paper towels.
Repeat until all papdis are made. They can be stored for a few weeks if kept in an airtight container.

Prepare the Toppings
Gather the ingredients.
Wash, peel, and dice the potatoes.
In a medium-sized pot, add the potatoes and enough water to just cover the potatoes. Boil until fork tender.
Drain and set aside.
Next, in a small pot, add the chickpeas and enough water to just cover the chickpeas. Boil until fork tender.
Drain and place into a small bowl.
Using a fork or a masher, mash the chickpeas together with a dash of salt to a coarse texture.
Assemble and Serve

To serve, first set up all ingredients -- papdis, toppings, and chutneys -- within easy reach.

Dip 5 to 6 papdis per person into the yogurt. Then arrange on a plate.

Put a little potato, chickpeas, onion, and tomato on each Papdi.

When all are done in this way, drizzle a teaspoonful each of tamarind chutney and mint-coriander chutney on each papdi.

Sprinkle a handful of sev all over the papdis on the plate.

Then sprinkle red chili powder, cumin powder, and black rock salt and garnish with chopped coriander leaves.

Serve as soon as possible or the papdis will get soggy.

NAAN (LEAVENED INDIAN FLATBREAD)

Total: 2 hrs 5 mins
Prep: 2 hrs
Cook: 5 mins
Yield: 4 servings

Ingredients
1 1/2 tsp. dry yeast
1 cup warm water
1 1/2 tsp. sugar
3 cups all-purpose flour
1 tsp. salt (or to taste)
6 tbsp. ghee (clarified butter, divided)
3 tbsp. unsweetened yogurt
2 or 3 splashes vegetable cooking oil (or canola or sunflower oil)
3 tsp. onion seeds

Steps to Make It
Gather the ingredients.

Add the dry yeast and sugar to the warm water and stir till the yeast is dissolved. Cover and leave aside for 10 minutes or until the mixture begins to froth. This indicates the yeast is active. Keep aside.

Mix the flour and salt to taste and sift through a very fine sieve. Put it into a large mixing bowl and now add the yeast mixture, 3 tablespoons of ghee, and all the yogurt.

Use your fingertips to mix all this into a soft dough. Once mixed, flour a clean, flat surface (like your kitchen counter), and knead the dough till it is smooth and stretchy (elastic).

Grease a large bowl with a few drops of vegetable/ canola/ sunflower cooking oil and put the dough in it. Cover with cling wrap and allow to rest for about 90 minutes or till the dough doubles in volume.

Punch the dough down and knead again for 10 minutes.

Equally, divide the dough and roll between your palms to form 8 round balls.

Lightly flour the same surface on which you kneaded the dough and roll out each ball until you have a circle, 7 to 8 inches in diameter (1/2-inch thick). Gently pull on one edge of the circle to form the Naan into a teardrop shape. Do not pull too hard or you may tear the Naan. Instead of rolling the dough out (with a rolling pin) you can also pat it into a circle with your hands.

Preheat your oven 400 F / 200 C / Mark 6.

Lay a piece of aluminum foil on an oven tray (to cover) and grease it lightly with a few drops of cooking oil.

Place as many naans as will fit without touching each other on the tray.

Brush each naan with some ghee and sprinkle a pinch of onion seeds all over its surface.

Put the tray into the oven and cook till the naan begins to puff out and get lightly brown. Flip the Naan and repeat.

Remove from oven and serve hot in a foil-lined basket.

Enjoy!

☐

INDIAN KOFTA CURRY

Total: 65 mins
Prep: 45 mins
Cook: 20 mins
Yield: 6 servings

Ingredients
For the Kofta:
2 pounds (1 kilogram) beef mince
2 onions (chopped very fine)
2 tablespoons garlic paste
1 tablespoon ginger paste
2 tablespoons garam masala
3 tablespoons tomato ketchup
1/2 cup coriander leaves (chopped fine)
1/2 teaspoon salt
For the Gravy:
3 tablespoons vegetable cooking oil
3 onions (chopped very fine)
2 tablespoons garlic paste
1 tablespoon ginger paste

2 teaspoons coriander powder
1 teaspoon cumin powder
1/2 teaspoon turmeric powder
1 teaspoon chili powder
1 teaspoon garam masala
4 large tomatoes (cubed)
2 cups warm water
Salt to taste

Steps to Make It

Make the Kofta
Gather the ingredients.
Put the minced beef, chopped onions, garlic paste, ginger paste, garam masala, tomato ketchup, coriander leaves, and salt in a large bowl and mix well.
Ground meat for kofta meatballs.
Form the mixture into equal-sized balls and keep on a plate.
Shaped kofta meatballs.

Make the Gravy
Gather the ingredients.
Heat the oil in a pan and add the remaining chopped onions. Fry until they are light brown. Add the ginger paste and garlic paste. Fry for 1 minute.
Onions, garlic past and ginger in the frying pan.
Add all the powdered spices (coriander, cumin, red chili powder, garam masala, and turmeric) and fry for 2 to 3 minutes.
Kofta spices added to the frying pan.
Add the tomatoes and mix well. Fry the masala until the oil begins to separate from the onions and tomatoes.
Tomatoes added to the frying pan for kofta.
Add the warm water to the masala and season with salt to taste. Gently add the meatballs and let sit; do not stir for at least 5 minutes.
Kofta added to the masala to cook.
Stir gently so as not to break the meatballs.
Cook uncovered until the meatballs are done, about 10 minutes. The gravy can be as thick as you like, so feel free to add water or cook down gravy as needed.

Homemade kofta meatballs.
Serve with jeera rice and kachumbar salad and enjoy!
☐

AALOO (POTATO) PARATHA

Total: 2 hrs 10 mins
Prep: 70 mins
Cook: 60 mins
Yield: 4 portions (4 servings)

Ingredients
5 medium potatoes (boiled, peeled, and very well mashed)
2 teaspoon coriander powder
1 teaspoon cumin powder
1/2 teaspoon cumin seeds
1/2 teaspoon turmeric
1 teaspoon red chili powder
salt to taste
3 tablespoons coriander leaves (finely chopped)
1 piece ginger (2 inches, finely grated)
2 cups flour (whole wheat)
2 tablespoons vegetable oil (or sunflower or canola oil)

Steps to Make It

Put the mashed potatoes, coriander and cumin powders, cumin seeds, turmeric, chili powder, salt to taste, chopped fresh coriander and grated ginger into a large mixing bowl. Blend all ingredients well by stirring. Once well mixed, keep aside for later.

Put the flour, oil/ghee, and all the ingredients (except the water) into a large mixing bowl.

Rub together to form a crumbly mix.

Now slowly add water, a little at a time and knead well to make a smooth, pliable dough. Cover and set aside for an hour.

Divide the dough into golf ball-sized portions and roll between your hands till they are smooth and without cracks.

Very lightly flour a rolling board or clean counter surface and roll each ball into a 5 inch circle. Now take a tablespoon-full of the potato mix and spoon it into the center of the circle you just made. Slowly lift the edges and bring together in the center to form a pouch. Press the ends together tightly to close the pouch. Once sealed, press down gently to flatten so that you have a flattened pouch.

Lightly flour your rolling surface and roll this pouch into a 7 to 8 inch circle. Don't worry too much if the filling oozes out. This happens often but can be avoided by using a very light hand to roll out the paratha. Just gather up the filling and either keep aside or try to put it back into the paratha and pinch the dough to seal. Also, if you're just starting out with Aaloo Parathas, do not worry about getting the perfect round shape as it takes a little practice to achieve. Whatever the shape, it tastes just as good! For convenience roll out as many parathas as you like, stacking them, ready to cook with a layer of cling film between each paratha.

Heat a griddle and fry the parathas one at a time like this: Put a paratha on the griddle. Do the first flip when you see tiny bubbles rise on the surface of the paratha. As soon as the first flip is done, drizzle a bit of oil on the top and spread well over the surface of the paratha. Flip again in 30 seconds and drizzle oil on this surface too. The paratha is done when both sides are crispy and golden brown.

Serve with chilled yogurt and your favorite pickle or chutney.

☐

PALAK KI SUBZI

Total: 30 mins
Prep: 15 mins
Cook: 15 mins
Yield: 2-3 servings

Ingredients
2 bunches spinach (approximately 1 lb or 500 gms)
2 tbsps vegetable/ canola/ sunflower cooking oil
1 tsp cumin seeds
2 dry red chillies broken into 1" bits
8-10 cloves of garlic chopped very fine
1 large onion sliced very thin
1/2 tsp red chilli powder (reduce if you want less heat)
1/2 tsp turmeric powder
1/2 tsp raw mango powder (amchoor)
Salt to taste

Steps to Make It
Chop off the stems on the spinach close to the roots and throw roots away. Wash the spinach very well under running water till absolutely clean.

Drain fully (use a salad spinner if necessary) and then chop coarsely. Keep aside.

Heat the oil in a deep pan on a medium flame. When hot, add the cumin seeds and cook till they stop spluttering. Now add the dry red chilli and allow to cook for 30 seconds or till darker.

Add the finely chopped garlic and fry till it starts to turn a pale golden color. Now add the onions and fry till soft.

Add the spinach and mix well. Cook uncovered till the spinach wilts slightly.

Add all the spices and salt to taste. Stir well to mix all ingredients. Cook for another 3-4 minutes and turn fire off.

Serve hot with a lentil dish like Masala Daal and Chapatis (for a vegetarian meal) or Dahi Gosht (lamb in yoghurt sauce) and Chapatis (for a non-vegetarian meal).

☐

VEGETARIAN INDIAN PALAK PANEER WITH RICOTTA

Total:25 mins
Prep:10 mins
Cook:15 mins
Yield:4 servings

Ingredients
2 tbsp olive oil + 2 tbsp
2 cloves garlic, minced
1 onion, diced
1 tbsp fresh ginger, grated or minced
2 tsp cumin
1 tsp coriander

1/2 tsp turmeric

1/2 cup sour cream

3 large bunches of spinach

8 ounces fresh whole milk ricotta cheese, drained

dash salt, to taste

Steps to Make It

In a large saucepan over medium heat, sautee the garlic and the onion in 2 tablespoons of olive oil for a minute or two.

Add the fresh ginger, cumin, coriander and turmeric, stirring, and allow the spices to cook for another minute.

Next, reduce the heat to medium low and add the sour cream, stirring to combine, then the spinach. You may need to add the spinach a little bit at a time, waiting for it to cook down before adding more.

Allow the spinach to cook until done, about ten minutes.

In a separate skillet, using a spoon, scoop out the fresh ricotta into pre-heated oil one spoonful at a time.

Fry the ricotta in 2 tablespoons of olive oil until lightly browned.

Add the fried ricotta cheese to the spinach mixture.

Cover, and cook on medium low for 5 to 7 more minutes.

Add a dash of salt, to taste, and serve hot.

☐

VEGAN BROCCOLI AND TOFU IN GARLIC SAUCE RECIPE

Total: 20 mins
Prep: 5 mins
Cook: 15 mins
Yield: 3-4 servings

Ingredients
1 onion (diced)
4 cloves garlic (minced)
3 tablespoons olive oil
2 cups broccoli (chopped)
1 block firm or extra firm tofu (pressed)
1 1/2 teaspoon ginger powder
1/4 teaspoon cayenne pepper
3 tablespoon cornstarch
1/4 cup soy sauce
1 cup water

Steps to Make It
Prepare your tofu. Like most vegan tofu recipes, this one will taste best if you press the tofu.

Cut the tofu into 1-inch cubes.

Chop the broccoli, dice the onion, and mince the garlic.

In a large skillet, saute onions and garlic in olive oil until the onions turn clear, about 3 to 5 minutes.

Add the tofu, ginger, cayenne, and broccoli to the pan and continue to cook until broccoli is done, another 6 to 8 minutes.

In a separate small bowl, mix together the cornstarch, soy sauce, and water, then add this mixture to the broccoli and tofu.

Cook until sauce thickens, then remove from heat.

Serve the broccoli and tofu in garlic sauce over rice or whole grains and enjoy.

☐

VEGAN INDIAN PALAK "PANEER" (SPINACH AND TOFU)

Total: 20 mins
Prep: 10 mins
Cook: 10 mins
Yield: 4-6 servings

Ingredients
1 package tofu (firm or extra firm tofu, well pressed and sliced into 1-inch cubes)
2 tablespoons plus 1 tablespoon olive oil
3 cloves garlic (minced)
3 tablespoons curry powder
1 teaspoon turmeric
1 tablespoons cumin
1/4 teaspoon ginger powder
2 tablespoons water
1/3 cup soy yogurt (if you can't find plain, use vanilla or lemon)
6 bunches spinach

Steps to Make It

Gather the ingredients.

Drain and press your tofu well. Not sure how to do that? Check out this step by step guide for how to press tofu. Once your tofu is drained and pressed, slice it into about 1-inch cubes.

Saute tofu and garlic in two tablespoons of olive oil until tofu is lightly crisp on all sides, about 4 to 5 minutes.

In a separate large skillet or a wok, heat the other tablespoon of olive oil. Add the curry powder, turmeric, ginger powder, and water, then whisk in the non-dairy yogurt.

Add the spinach, stirring to cover in the yogurt sauce. Depending on the size of your pan, you may need to add the spinach in batches. It cooks down □uickly, so stay on it and keep adding more as quickly as possible to ensure a relatively even cooking time.

Once the spinach is fully cooked down, remove the pan from heat and process the spinach mixture in a food processor or blender until almost creamy (an immersion blender will be useful for this step, if you have one) or until it has a nice texture, keeping in mind that some more moisture will be absorbed as it cooks and cools.

Return the spinach to the skillet and add the sauteed tofu. Cook and stir until the tofu is well mixed with the spinach and the dish is completely heated through.

Serve your vegan palak and tofu dish along side plain steamed white or brown rice, or, mix it up a bit and accompany your homecooked meal with another whole grain, such as □uinoa or your favorite ancient grain.

□

CROCK POT INDIAN VEGETABLE CURRY RECIPE

Total: 6 hrs 10 mins
Prep: 10 mins
Cook: 6 hrs
Yield: 6 servings

Ingredients
3 potatoes (chopped)
1 cauliflower (chopped)
1 1/2 cups green peas
3 tomatoes (chopped)
3/4 teaspoon turmeric
1/2 teaspoon chili powder
1 1/2 teaspoon cumin
1 teaspoon curry
1 cup water

Steps to Make It
Gather the ingredients.
Place all ingredients in a crock pot or slow cooker.
Cook on low for 5 to 6 hours.
Serve and enjoy!

VEGETARIAN CHANA MASALA WITH SPINACH

Total: 25 mins
Prep: 5 mins
Cook: 20 mins
Yield: 3 servings

Ingredients
1/2 onion (diced)
3 cloves garlic (diced)
3 tablespoons olive oil
1 can (16 ounces) chickpeas (undrained, or 1 1/2 cups precooked chickpeas plus 1/2 cup water)
2 tablespoons lemon juice (juice from one lemon)
1/2 teaspoon curry powder
1/2 teaspoon coriander powder
1/2 teaspoon cumin
1/2 teaspoon garam masala
1 pound spinach (a large bunch or two handfuls, rinsed)

Steps to Make It

In a large skillet or frying pan, saute onions and garlic in olive oil until soft, about 3 to 5 minutes.

Add chickpeas straight from the can, including all the water.

Add lemon juice, curry powder, coriander powder, ground cumin, and garam masala. Simmer about 10 to 15 minutes, stirring occasionally, adding more water if needed until chickpeas are cooked and soft.

Reduce the heat, add spinach and cover. Allow spinach to wilt for 2 to 4 minutes.

Serve immediately and enjoy your chana masala.

A dish like this should be served with either plain white rice, simple Indian basmati rice, Indian lemon rice, or, if you want the extra protein boost, □uinoa. But another alternative is to serve it with warm Indian bread such as naan, roti, or chapati. Those are excellent for dipping into the mixture.

Refrigerate any leftovers and enjoy them within three to five days. Chana masala is perfect for freezing and taking to the office for lunch later, so make a double batch if you'd like. It will retain the best □uality in the freezer for three to six months and reheats easily in the microwave. Be sure to label the container with the date and contents.

For a heartier chana masala, toss in some tofu with the chickpeas and serve over rice.
□

RAJMA DAL: RED KIDNEY BEAN CURRY

Total: 25 mins
Prep: 10 mins
Cook: 15 mins
Yield: 4 to 6 servings

Ingredients
2 tablespoons oil (vegetable, canola, or sunflower cooking oil)
1 teaspoon cumin seeds
2 medium onions (chopped finely)
2 inches ginger (julienned)
6 cloves garlic (minced)
2 green chilies (fresh, chopped fine)
2 large tomatoes (chopped into 1-inch cubes)
2 teaspoons coriander (powder)
1 teaspoon cumin (powder)
1 teaspoon garam masala
1/4 teaspoon turmeric (powder)
2 (15.5 oz.) cans red kidney beans (drained, rinsed under running water)
3 cups water (warm)
Salt to taste
1 pinch of asafetida

Garnish: coriander (chopped)

Steps to Make It

In a deep pan, heat the oil and add the cumin seeds. When they stop sizzling, add the onion and fry until soft.

Add the ginger and garlic and fry for 2 minutes.

Add the green chilies, tomatoes, coriander, cumin, turmeric, and garam masala and fry until the oil separates from the masala.

Add the red kidney beans, warm water, and asafetida, as well as the salt to taste. Cook until the beans are soft, approximately 10 minutes.

Mash some of the beans roughly to thicken the sauce.

Garnish with coriander and serve hot with rice, Kachumbar salad, and the pickle of your choice.

☐

MUTTER PANEER - PEAS AND COTTAGE CHEESE CURRY

Total: 45 mins
Prep: 15 mins
Cook: 30 mins
Yield: 4-6 servings

Ingredients
2 large onions (cut into quarters)
3 medium-sized tomatoes (cut into quarters)
6 tablespoons vegetable oil (or canola or sunflower cooking oil, divided)
1 pound paneer (cubed)
1 tablespoon ginger paste
2 tablespoons garlic paste
2 teaspoons coriander powder
1 teaspoon cumin powder
1/2 tsp turmeric powder
2 teaspoons garam masala
2 green chillies (finely chopped)
1/2 pound shelled peas
1 1/2 cups water (hot)
Salt (to taste)
3 tablespoons heavy cream

Garnish: 1/3 cup fresh coriander leaves (finely chopped)

Steps to Make It
Ingredients for mutter paneer peas cottage cheese
Grind the onions into a fine paste in a food processor. Keep aside.
Next grind tomatoes into a fine paste and keep aside.
Heat 2 to 3 tablespoons of the vegetable oil in a deep pan and gently stir-fry the cubes of paneer till golden.
When golden, remove onto a paper towel and keep aside.
In the same vessel, heat the remaining 2 to 3 tablespoons of the vegetable oil and add the onion paste. Fry till it turns light brown. You will need to stir fre☐uently to avoid the paste burning. Also, do not over-fry as it will turn bitter and ruin the curry. Another hassle-free way to do this is to chop the onions fine and then sauté till pale golden, then grind in the food processor.
When the onion paste is fried, add tomato paste, ginger and garlic paste, and sauté for another 2 minutes.
Next, add the coriander, cumin, turmeric, and garam masala powders, and the finely chopped green chilies and sauté, stirring continuously, till the cooking oil begins to separate from the masala (spice mixture).
Now add the peas to the masala and fry for 2 to 3 minutes.
Then add the previously fried paneer, hot water, and salt, to taste, reduce the heat to a simmer and cook till the gravy thickens.
When the gravy is as thick as you would like, turn off the heat and stir in the cream.
Garnish with coriander leaves and serve with chapati, paratha, naan, or jeera rice.
☐

PUNJABI-STYLE CHOLE CHICKPEA CURRY RECIPE

Total: 65 mins
Prep: 20 mins
Cook: 45 mins
Yield: 4 servings

Ingredients
3 large onions (sliced thin, divided)
2 large tomatoes (chopped)
1 tablespoon ginger paste
2 tablespoons garlic paste
2 tablespoons vegetable oil (or canola or sunflower cooking oil)
2 bay leaves
5 to 6 cloves
3 to 4 green cardamoms
5 to 6 peppercorns
1 teaspoon cumin powder
2 teaspoons coriander powder
1/2 teaspoon red chili powder
1/4 teaspoon turmeric powder
2 teaspoons garam masala
2 cans of chickpeas

Kosher salt (to taste)
Water (enough to make a gravy)
1-inch piece of ginger (julienned)
2 tablespoons fresh coriander leaves (chopped fine)

Steps to Make It
Grind 2 of the sliced onions, the tomatoes, and the ginger and garlic paste together into a smooth paste in a food processor.
Heat the vegetable oil in a deep, thick-bottomed pan on medium heat.
Add the bay leaves, cloves, cardamom, and peppercorns and sauté until slightly darker and mildly fragrant.
Add the remaining sliced onion and fry until light golden in color.
Add the onion-tomato paste you made earlier and fry till the oil begins to separate from the paste.
Add the dry, powdered spices—cumin, coriander, red chili, turmeric, and garam masala powders. Sauté, stirring fre□uently, for 5 more minutes.
Drain the water in the can from the chickpeas and rinse them well under running water.
Now add the chickpeas to the masala you fried up earlier. Stir to mix everything well.
Add salt to taste and enough hot water to make the gravy—about 1 1/2 cups.
Simmer and cook covered for 10 minutes.
Use a flat spoon or potato masher to mash some of the chickpeas coarsely. Stir to mix everything well.
Garnish with juliennes of ginger and finely chopped fresh coriander leaves. A s□ueeze of lemon and a handful of very finely chopped onion tastes great as a garnish too.
Serve hot and enjoy!
□

KADHAI GOSHT

Total: 3 hrs 30 mins
Prep: 3 hrs 15 mins
Cook: 15 mins
Yield: 6-8 servings

Ingredients
1 kg lamb/ mutton cut into 2" pieces
1 cup yogurt
2 tbsps garlic paste
2 tbsps lemon juice
2 tsps garam masala (see link below for recipe to make your own)
Salt to taste
3 tbsps vegetable/ canola/ sunflower cooking oil
4 green chillies slit lengthwise
2 tsps coriander powder
1 tsp cumin powder
2 medium tomatoes chopped fine
Ginger julliennes to garnish
Fresh chopped corainder to garnish

Steps to Make It
Gather the ingredients.
Mix the lamb/ mutton with the yogurt, garlic paste, lemon juice, garam masala and salt to taste, cover and allow to marinate for 3 hours.

Heat the oil in a Kadhai (or any other wok-like pan) on a medium flame. Add the green chillies and fry till they stop spluttering.

Add the lamb with its marinade and fry, stirring frequently, for 5-7 minutes.

Now add the tomatoes, corainder and cumin powder and mix well. Sprinkle some water over the meat, cover, simmer the flame and cook till the meat is done. Check occassionally and add more water if needed to prevent sticking and burning. Ideally this dish has a minimal amount of thick gravy.

Turn off fire, garnish with ginger and coriander leaves and serve with hot Chapatis (Indian flatbread) or Naans.

Printed in Great Britain
by Amazon